FESTIVALS OF PATIENCE

FESTIVALS OF PATIENCE

The Verse Poems of Arthur Rimbaud
Translated by Brian Kim Stefans
Chicago: Kenning Editions
2021

TABLE OF CONTENTS

FOREWARD

by Jennifer Moxley

A visionary translation of a great poet from a foreign past records an amatory sympathy between a living writer and a dead one. In this convergence the poems are threaded through by the translator's sensibilities and revivified into a language they never intended to speak. It is a kind of magic. Yet the specter of the "original" threatens to haunt even a compelling translation out of the house of literature. That is why I agree with French poet Emmanuel Hocquard when he writes that the goal, perhaps quixotic, is to create a work that becomes a part of the literature of the target language, but could never have been written by a native of that tongue (*Ca, jamais un poète française ne l'aurait écrit*).* In which case, the book before you would give us an Arthur Rimbaud who, while fluent in American English, wrote poems unlike any written by a late nineteenth century American poet. This is precisely what Brian Kim Stefans has achieved in *Festivals of Patience*.

Many pious things are said about the work of literary translation, which is nerve-wracking and thankless. Around every corner linguistically agile pedants of the literal await to wag fingers, as if every decision the translator makes must stand up in a court of law. "If you don't want to make mistakes, don't do translations." This, according to Kate Briggs's charming essay on translation, *The Little Art*, is an "enabling dictum" someone once gave her. Good advice. Yet the word "mistake" seems to imply a fixity in language and word-meanings quite out of keeping with the fluid art of poetry and translation. Strictly speaking the word "cat" in English is the equivalent of the word "*chat*" in French. But rare is the poet who speaks *strictly*. One of the

---

* *49 + 1 nouveaux poètes américains.* Un bureau sur l'Atlantique Series, Éditions Royaumont (1991).

unfortunate conditions of offering up a new translation of a famous text is the supposed necessity of justifying your labor by denigrating that of your quondam peers. I hope never to meet a translator motivated only by a cussed mission to "set the record straight."

If translation is, as implied by my opening sentence, a form of love, then translating all the verse poems of a poet as demanding, bickered over, and coveted as Arthur Rimbaud might constitute an *amour fou.* Anyone who undertakes such a task takes the double risk of destroying their love and arousing a jealous army of the spurned. For Rimbaud is one of those cultish poets petulant counter-cultural misfits feel singularly possessive of. I know, because I'm one of them and that's how I feel. This "haunting young man," as I called him in my memoir, was a youthful infatuation of mine. Imagine, therefore, the delicious surprise and singular pleasure I felt when rendezvousing with this work, so many years later, in Stefans's beautiful renderings, and falling in love all over again.

I suppose I shouldn't have been surprised. Brian Kim Stefans has always been a bit of a charming brat, too smart for his own good. He chews on thought-bones like a frothed-up cur and argues with the skills of a barrister. Which make his sensibilities a dream match for the precocious Communard energy and pungent pathos of Arthur Rimbaud's brilliant and varied poems in verse. Stefans's chaotic process, as described in his introduction, of madly typing and then revising, willy-nilly, in raucous Los Angeles bars, allowed him to somatically channel Rimbaud's signature torpor and impatience, which Kristen Ross identifies as the rhythm of adolescence. One of the things that puzzles people about Rimbaud is how a kid could write so well and with so much insight. This shouldn't be a puzzle at all: unconstrained by compromise, yet able to see its approach, adolescents may have a window of vision that closes when we "mature" into propertied lives. It is necessary to draw the shades, lest we unravel civilization.

Though the teenage poet skewers bourgeois hypocrisy and complacency in his poems, Stefans makes a helpful corrective to the too-simple construction of Rimbaud as nothing more than a nihilistic punk. He reminds us that

Rimbaud's ultimate vision for the future poet is civic minded, materialistic, and infused with a classical love for order. "In Rimbaud's mind, poets are not just *seers*, they are cosmic citizens," Stefans writes. This is also where we encounter the feminist Rimbaud, who asserted that women would never be poets until they became citizens, until they were freed from their "endless servitude" to men.

Rimbaud was a formally restless writer, whose style developed and changed so rapidly it can be difficult to see the cohesiveness of his work from one phase to the next. Stefans's translation is remarkable in that it succeeds in giving us a vision of the whole poet. As Rimbaud moves from schoolboy imitations of Horace, to political fantasias of destruction and scatological heresies, Stefans's American English maintains his prickly diction, extraordinary painterly images, odiferous details (has there ever been a poet who made you *smell* the world so much?), and vibrating restless subjectivity.

I applaud Stefans's decision to sometimes leave Rimbaud's words in the original. I was delighted, for example, to come across "water lily" left as the French "*nénuphar*," a word I have always loved. In his translation of the "Seer Letter," included as an appendix, Stefans chooses not to translate the word *informe* (typically rendered as "formlessness") in the passage where Rimbaud assigns the future poet a daunting task: "A language must be found." Stefans's decision allows us to hear how Rimbaud's word, *informe*, resonates with Gerard Manley Hopkins's concepts of *inscape* and *instress*—forms that inform the world, rather than impose upon it—the secret doctrine which underlies New American poetry's preference for organic form over *vers libre*. Thus Stefans gently nudges Rimbaud away from the Beat poets and rock stars, and closer to minds like Robert Duncan, Denise Levertov, and Charles Olson, all of whom envisioned a future for the poet as "cosmic citizen," participating in the forms of a moral universe.

In closing I would like to note that, while Stefans's translations capture Rimbaud's prelapsarian yearnings, old-world decay, snotty ageism, and heretical takedowns, they do so in a way that allows us to feel the sympathetic and sad heart beating beneath it all. Yes, Rimbaud the gangly bedraggled half-man/half child was infamously anti-social and supposedly depraved, but Rimbaud the poet, the *vâtes*, was a delicate wordsmith with exquisite manners and sensibilities that invite us *not* into the violence of his mind, but into the violence of the post-Enlightenment European world. Stefans brings to life Rimbaud's bookish elegance and street speech in taut and vivid poetic lines, making *Festivals of Patience* the best translation of these poems since Paul Schmidt's of the late 1960s.

INTRODUCTION

The greatness of Rimbaud is to have led poetry to the failure of poetry.
—Georges Bataille

French poet Jean Nicolas Arthur Rimbaud (October 20, 1854 – November 10, 1891) is known not just only for the innovative, often subversive, nature of his poetry, but for a few key facts about his life.

Born and raised in the provincial town of Charleville in the Ardennes, Rimbaud composed his first poems when he was fourteen. Written in Latin, these early efforts were for classroom assignments, but nonetheless demonstrated the poet's extraordinary technical ability and wild, visionary and highly literate imagination as a teenager. He won local awards for these poems, many of which appeared in *Le Moniteur de L'Enseignement secondaire*, a publication devoted to the finest work by students in the region. Two poems in French, "The Orphans' New Year's Gifts" and "The First Evening," were published on January 2, 1870 and August 20, 1870 respectively, the only two works of his to appear in France while he still lived in the country with the exception of *Une saison en enfer* ("A Season in Hell,"), a prose poem and one of his most famous works, which he published at his own expense with a Belgian printer in 1873.

When he first started writing poems in French, Rimbaud was aspiring to be among the "Parnassians," a group of Parisian poets who sought to distance themselves from the "subjective"—sentimental, unduly political—aspect of French Romantic poetry and aim for a highly formal, even marmoreal, perfection in their verse. He sent three poems to Théodore de Banville, one of the leaders of the Parnassians, on May 24, 1870 for inclusion in the final issue of *Le Parnasse contemporain* ("The Contemporary Parnassus"), including the long poem "Credo in unam," which he hoped would become the "creed" of the Parnassians. But Rimbaud, even when still living in the provinces, soon made an abrupt turn against their stances and aesthetics—indeed, to the degree of mocking these poets outright. After several attempts to reach Paris, either by train or on foot, he responded to an invitation from the twenty-seven-year-old poet Paul Verlaine to stay with him and his young pregnant wife, Mathilde. Rimbaud was just shy of seventeen when Verlaine described him as having "[t]he real head of a child, chubby and fresh, on a big, bony, rather clumsy body of a still-growing adolescent." What ensued is the most infamous relationship—literary, emotional, sexual—ever to occur among poets.

Verlaine soon left his wife to take up an itinerant, often volatile, existence with his new acolyte. Anecdotes about Rimbaud's life during this time in Paris are legion. The poet indulged in absinthe, opium and hashish, and gained a reputation for being rude, unbathed and lice-ridden. Furthermore, Verlaine (who returned to, but as suddenly left, his wife a few times during this period, and who often returned to a devout Catholicism when times got rough) and Rimbaud flaunted their close relationship in public, inspiring rumors about the nature of their affair.

Two incidents regarding Rimbaud during this period are emblematic. The first, known as the "Carjat Incident," occurred at a dinner held on March 2, 1872 among the "Vilains Bonshommes," a group of writers and artists associated with the Parnassians. As biographer Graham Robb relates:

> As usual, the most tedious poets took the longest time. Rimbaud bit his tongue and waited for the end. Then a justly forgotten poet named Auguste Creisels stood up and started to recite his "Sonnet du combat": a pompous attempt at wit which evidently caused its author great satisfaction.

> Rimbaud began to add an extra syllable to the end of each line:

> Subject to this law, the uniform tercet—*merde!*
> Stands grave and rigid at its designated post—*merde!*

What happened next is not completely clear, but the general idea is the same in every account. The poet-photographer Étienne Carat called Rimbaud a "little toad." Rimbaud reached back behind him, grabbed Verlaine's swordstick and lunged at Carjat across the table, grazing his hand. Rimbaud was disarmed, raised off the floor by the barrel-chested Carjat and dumped in the hall outside.*

This act of literary terrorism is mirrored in the acidic parodies Rimbaud contributed to the "Album Zutique," a collection of bawdy satires by Rimbaud and his friends, around this time. Carjat, incidentally, is the photographer who took the most famous portrait of Rimbaud—seeming to stare out into the distant cosmos with his pale blue eyes—that has appeared on countless book covers over the years (and which is absent on this one).

The other anecdote concerns a painting called "Un coin de table" (often translated as "By the Table") by the artist Henri Fantin-Latour of the attendees, including Rimbaud and Verlaine, of the irregular meetings of the Parnassians. Fantin-Latour was forced to replace the head of the poet Albert Mérat with a vase of flowers because Mérat "would not be painted with pimps and thieves."

Rimbaud's experiments with drugs, seeming to fulfill his advocation of the *"rational disordering* of *all the senses"* as he stated in one of his "Letters of the Seer," his visceral hatred for anything resembling 19th-century bourgeois norms, his virulent anti-clericalism (after a youth of extreme piety), his travels with Verlaine throughout Europe and the torrid nature of their relationship—toward the end of which Verlaine was sentenced to two years in prison after shooting Rimbaud in the hand—have become part of his legend.

Rimbaud gave up poetry around the age of twenty-one, soon after the composition of *Une saison en enfer* and a series, *Illuminations*, which were

---

* *Rimbaud: A Biography.* New York: W. W. Norton & Company, 2001.

largely in prose but which included what are often considered the first examples of *vers libre*, "free verse," in European poetry. After several trips to England and vagabonding in several countries in Europe, Rimbaud became a trader in Africa while contributing several articles to French geography journals during the period of French colonial expansion. This is the final element of Rimbaud's "legend": the great "silence" of his later years during which he wrote no poetry, as far as we know, and cared not at all for his burgeoning reputation in Paris after Verlaine had published several poems—"The Drunken Boat" and "Vowels" among them—and parts of *Illuminations* in literary journals. These publications caused an immediate sensation.

Rimbaud died in Marseille at the age of thirty-seven, having had his leg amputated from what was determined, post-mortem, to be bone cancer. His sister, Isabelle, who was with him during his final weeks, and who didn't know he had written poetry, wrote to their mother: "He is fair, a saint, a martyr, one of God's elect." Isabelle's claims that Rimbaud had made a deathbed return to Christianity are almost certainly untrue.

Note on the Translations

The translations in this volume started with a naive intuition: that one could create English versions of Rimbaud's version poems following the metrical patterns of the originals. The challenge was to reproduce the syllable counts in the French—12-syllables for the alexandrines, various syllable counts for the ballad forms and others Rimbaud invented—in English. I never imagined that I could reproduce the rhyme schemes strictly, which I thought would make my translations pedantic, not to mention ugly, but I wanted the ghost of these patterns present. These formal constraints, which I sometimes followed robotically, were intended to restrict whatever urge I might have had to render these poems as "free verse" or to let them gravitate toward the stress patterns that form the basis for English-language formal poetry.

The alexandrine in English poetry has only been used sparingly. Michael Drayton's *Poly-Olbion* (published in two parts in 1612 and 1622) is the longest English poem written entirely in rhyming alexandrines, but because it adheres to a 6-stress pattern with predictable caesura in its nearly 15,000 lines, it gets a bit tedious. Edmund Spenser masterfully employed it as the final line of each stanza of his epic poem *The Faerie Queene* (1596), but by 1711 Alexander Pope in his *An Essay on Criticism* decried its use as a sort of stentorian punctuation to iambic pentameter paragraphs: "A needless alexandrine ends the song, / That, like a wounded snake, drags its slow length along." Percy Bysshe Shelley and Thomas Hardy effectively used the line to close each stanza of their "To a Skylark" and "The Convergence of the Twain" respectively. Robert Browning's extraordinary "Fifine at the Fair" (1872) might be the most recent English long poem—a monologue in 132 parts in the voice of Molière's Don Juan—written entirely in alexandrines.

If there's a contribution I can make to this tradition, it's that I've discarded any concern with stress pattern, particularly iambic, rendering the lines instead in syllabics that can verge on prose, somewhat in the manner of William Carlos Williams, Marianne Moore or the poets of the New York School. As for rhyme, I've often employed any variation that seemed suitable to give the *effect* of rhyme—off-rhymes, slant-rhymes, internal rhymes, masculine (stressed) endings rhymed with feminine (unstressed) endings, and even on occasion an "eye rhyme" (words that are spelled similarly, but are pronounced differently)—providing each couplet and stanza something of the sense of closure, and of course the pleasure, that rhyme normally gives.

I also created other basic rules. For example, if Rimbaud repeated a line or a phrase in its entirety, I repeated my translation of that part as well. I also only occasionally offered a gloss within a poem to help the reader—I render "Gambier" as "Gambier pipe" for example. But for the most part, if the poem was difficult to understand by a French reader in the original, I permitted it (while aiming as much as I could for an accurate translation) to be difficult in the English.

Outside of that, writing these translations was largely a matter of "going on my nerve" in Frank O'Hara's phrase from his playful 1959 manifesto, "Personism." I would sit down at my typewriter and write slowly, counting out syllables with my fingers, and leaving a gap in the middle of the alexandrine to insure adherence to the French caesura that normally appears after the 6th syllable.* After scanning the poems into my computer and making a few revisions, I would post the draft to Facebook, largely so that I could revise it as I went about my days and nights. I often found myself working on my translations in odd locations, like at the legendary bar Frolic Room on Hollywood Boulevard amidst whatever chaos reigned around me among my friends and the often strange, vibrant creatures who patronized the place. In this way, I would have to hear the translation, which, naturally, I very much wanted to be a *poem*, amidst the sorts of dins and cackles that Rimbaud himself might have heard at L'Univers or Cabaret-Vert.

I'm afraid, given some liberties I have taken, that some might not consider these renderings "translations." Naturally, I disagree. My first argument would be that adherence to the syllable counts of the originals without concern for stress patterns—six strong stresses per 12-syllable line, as in many of the poems I cite above— points to a *fidelity*, not vulnerable to personal taste or fickleness, toward a central *content* of any poem, especially one written in meters. It might be "formal" or "mathematical," in a sense, but nonetheless is it something that's *true* about the source poem that is otherwise obscured by free verse translations.

This method also opens up the possibility in English poetry for something like a "French line" in which rhythm is expressed more like subterranean pulses, characterized the by the length of vowel sounds, rather than

---

* In French prosody, no word should bridge this caesura, a rule Verlaine was one of the first to break and which Rimbaud, even before he had met Verlaine, found delightful. Rimbaud wrote to his friend Georges Izambard that Verlaine's volume *Fêtes Galantes* was "extremely strange, very funny; but really, it's adorable" and quoted a line from the volume expressly to note how Verlaine had broken this rule:

Et la tigresse épou / vantable d'Hyrcanie

Rimbaud noted that this was an act of "serious license."

through definitive beats. Even the most avant-garde of the early Anglophone modernists, such as Ezra Pound and T.S. Eliot, were indebted to a heavily-stressed line. Some of Pound's earliest "free verse" poems, such as "The Return" or his quasi-translation of the Anglo-Saxon "The Seafarer," embraced this quality of the English language; he often performed "The Seafarer" beating a drum to emphasize it. Eliot argued in "Reflections on *Vers Libre*" that "the ghost of some simple metre should lurk behind the arras in even the 'freest' verse; to advance menacingly as we doze, and withdraw as we rouse." By this, he could only mean stress pattern.

An example from my translations might clarify what I mean. In the following, from "The Sleeper in the Valley," I do, in fact, write a line that could be considered iambic pentameter:

Il dort dans le soleil, la main sur sa poitrine
Tranquille. Il a deux trous rouges au côté droit.

He basks in the sun, an idle hand on his breast
—tranquil. Two red cavities yawn on his right side.

In this case, my allegiance was to the enjambment of the original—"tranquille" finds its same place in the translation, though in my instance, after an em-dash. I translate the plural form of the word "trou"—which is unambiguously the word "hole" (a word Rimbaud uses quite often, for instance in "The Astonished," in which I use the word "hole" every time it appears) as "cavities" because of sound patterning. The word "trou" actually appears twice in "The Sleeper in the Valley," and for many this is one its most intriguing aspects as the first "trou" describes the "vale" (in my translation) where the soldier lies, and the second, the gunshot wounds. But I couldn't find a way to repeat the word effectively and maintain a sonic integrity in the translation. The word "yawn" is an embellishment, but as with all of my revisions, it only occurred as a result of what I call a close *hearing* of the line.

In a few cases, I reversed the ordering of lines. For instance, the final three lines of "Tartuffe's Punishment" run:

Donc, il se confessait, priait, avec un râle!
L'homme se contenta d'emporter ses rabats...
—Peuh! Tartufe était nu du haut jusques en bas!

So, he confessed—he prayed—he shook a death rattle!
Buck naked, wow!—Tartuffe froze like a mannequin.
And the man, self-possessed, walked off with the clothes pile.

After playing around with the translation, it finally struck me that Rimbaud's final image of Tartuffe standing naked on the road wasn't funny enough to act as the final twist of the knife against this religious hypocrite. This could just signal a difference in the nature of French and American senses of humor. "Mannequin" is, of course, another embellishment.

Occasionally, a motif would appear in a translation that didn't appear in Rimbaud's poem. For instance, following is my translation of the final stanza of "The Drunken Boat":

Je ne puis plus, baigné de vos langueurs, ô lames,
Enlever leur sillage aux porteurs de cotons,
Ni traverser l'orgueil des drapeaux et des flammes,
Ni nager sous les yeux horribles des pontons.

Never again can I, oh waves, embalmed in sleep,
ride fast into the wakes of English cotton boats
nor cross nations' borders, their torches, flags, and keeps
nor swim by prison hulks that taunt me with their ropes.

There are no "ropes" in the last verse of Rimbaud's poem, but we know, reading "Dance of the Hanging Man" and "The Blacksmith," that Rimbaud certainly had intimations of the gallows. My translation, through its twists and turns, flows and eddies, elevates the status of ropes—"the lines from my haulers slackened," "churning in whirlpools keel, rudder and line," "sickly pallor / of drowned men flicked my ropes," and so forth, so it didn't strike me as an impertinence to return to the motif.

The notion of being "embalmed in sleep," as opposed to being merely "bathed in your languors" ("baigné de vos langueurs") reflects back on "un noyé pensif" earlier in the poem (it also harkens back to "Sisters of Charity"). But what is most important to me—and it was a discovery myself as I wrote the translation—is that "The Drunken Boat" is a journey of surprises across a pattern of regularities, which is to say, the journey is somehow always "forward" even as it leads you across travesties of consciousness, of deep abysses, of unasked-for profundities. English alexandrines actually accentuate this aspect: given the long but regular line, one encounters surprises that don't break the flow so much as accentuate the dangers of departing from predictability. Every word of "The Drunken Boat" can't be a revelation—the surprises are animated against a regular pattern.

The stanza that most surprised me, in writing the translation, is the following: quite quiet, seemingly brief, departing from the apparent chaos of discovery, yet meditative and maintaining the syllable count, which is the role the penultimate stanza plays in Rimbaud's poem:

> Si je désire une eau d'Europe, c'est la flache
> Noire et froide où vers le crépuscule embaumé
> Un enfant accroupi plein de tristesses, lâche
> Un bateau frêle comme un papillon de mai.

> If there is a water of Europe that I crave
> it is a black puddle, cold, in sweet-smelling night
> where a sad child, squatting, sets forth upon its way
> a folded boat, fragile as a May butterfly.

My only insertion, here, is the note that the boat is "folded"—I was imagining a paper boat. I write this only to illustrate the limits of when my translations were "creative" or "accurate" in the sense that a translation of a legal document, or a work of philosophy, would have to be tied *indexically* to an original. My argument is that translations of poetry don't work backwards by *necessity* to the original text—there's not chain of A to B that can be followed backwards from B to A in a poem since a poem's form confers meaning on the text in a way that doesn't appear in prose such as legal documents and (most) philosophy. I could be right or wrong in my judgments along these lines, but I also don't think that previous translators of Rimbaud, the very many of them, satisfy this stricture much better than I have.

The Letters of the Seer

I've decided to append to this volume my own translations of the two "Letters of the Seer," Rimbaud's only substantial statements about what he was trying to do in his poems. Written when he was still sixteen, these two letters, especially the second one, are are among the greatest aesthetic manifestos ever written. Despite their brevity, there are a number of conceptual—not to mention tonal and linguistic—elements in them that the reader has to struggle with to give them an easy coherence.

"Je est une autre," which I render here as "I is an other," is among the most famous statements from the letters, arguing for a final break with anything like Romantic "subjectivity" and, instead, for an understanding of the mind and body as participating in the *immanence* of worldly self-creation—as part of the *non-conscious* movement of matter and, perhaps, spirit. The poet is no longer human in the newfound sense of the Romantics, but rather is *divested* of ego. He could be said to become an "object" among the many objects of the world, suggesting that what Rimbaud meant by "objective poetry"—an aim of the Parnassians—wasn't merely that a poet should take a scientific stance toward reality, but treat the *self* as mere *matter*. In the first letter, the poet is "wood which finds itself a violin," and in the second, brass that "wakes up a trumpet."

Equally famous is his declaration that "[t]he Poet makes himself a *seer* by a long, gigantic and *rational disordering* of *all the senses*." The key word in this statement, "dérèglement," is often translated as "derangement," which certainly is more flavorful than "disordering." However, it gives the mistaken impression that one can *derange*—cause to become insane—a single *sense*, not to mention *all* of them. One can disorder a deck of cards, meaning subject them to a chance arrangement, but one can't *derange* them. While it's true that Rimbaud wrote that, after the poet has acquired his visions, he might, indeed, go insane—"[though] he ends up by losing the intelligence of his visions, he has seen them!"—it's inaccurate to say that Rimbaud wants poets to go insane to attain these visions. "Dérèglement" might also be translated as "deregulation" given its root in the word "règlement," which can mean "rule" or "regulation," but given that "order" itself suggests that there is a dominant if invisible "rule," I've stuck with "disordering."

What is less noticed in the letters, written just before the "Bloody Week" starting May 21st, 1871 when the French army massacred thousands of Communards,* is how much of Rimbaud's visionary plan is tied to a *civic* sense—that the verses and lyres of the time of the Greeks "*rhythment l'Action*" ("give rhythm to Action").

For all of the adoption by later poets, especially Anglophone, of Rimbaud as the spokesperson for the marginal—of overlooked, even detested, segments of society, an ethos the Beat poets expressed so well—Rimbaud instead figures the poet as *central* to a society's progress. "The poet would define the amount of the unknown awakening in the universal soul of his time: he would give more—than the formulation of his thought, than the record of *his march toward Progress!* Enormity becoming the norm, absorbed by all, he would really be a *multiplier of progress!*" The poet makes manifest, in the poems, a sort of new *order* that will be of benefit to humankind: "Always filled with *Number* and *Harmony*, these poems will be made to endure. [...] Eternal art would have its functions; as poets are citizens. Poetry will not give rhythm to action, it *will be in advance.*" While much of this, of course, is subject to interpretation, I'd like to highlight this "civic" responsibility as a gloss on Rimbaud's own relationship to the Paris Commune, for which he

---

* "One of the first cataclysms to be chronicled by *The Times*, in its 20th year, was the brutal suppression of the Paris Commune by French and Prussian troops during the "Bloody Week" in May 1871. The most conservative estimates have placed the number of dead at 6,000 to 7,000. The Encylopaedia Britannica states that about 20,000 insurrectionists were killed. Other estimates reach 30,000." "1871 | 'The Paris Agony'," *The New York Times*, Nov. 19, 2015.

wrote, as best he could, "creeds" or anthems much as he had tried to write one for the Parnassians earlier on.

Rimbaud is most typically Romantic when he is looking back to the Greeks as providing the most pure expression of poetry. As Shelley wrote in "A Defense of Poetry" in 1819: "Horace, Catullus, Ovid, and generally the other great writers of the Vergilian age, saw man and nature in the mirror of Greece. The institutions also, and the religion of Rome, were less poetical than those of Greece, as the shadow is less vivid than the substance." However, Rimbaud can be seen as the first Modernist in that he doesn't mark a decline from the age of Greece, rather, he dismisses almost everything written since then, stating that after the Greeks "music and rhymes are games, pastimes… Universal intelligence has always naturally hurled out its ideas; men picked up a part of these fruits of the mind: people acted through them, wrote books about them: things continued thus, man not working on himself, not yet being awake, or not yet in the fullness of the great dream. Civil servants, writers: author, creator, poet, that man never existed!" He takes a machine gun not just to the 17th-century dramatist and poet Jean Racine, among the most universally recognized great French writers, but, in his closing paragraphs of the second letter, nearly the entirety of French poetry of his time. In Rimbaud's mind, poets are not just seers, they are cosmic citizens—anything less is nonsense.

My one innovation in my translation of the letters is in the following passage from the letter to Paul Demeny written on May 15, 1871:

> Il est chargé de l'humanité, des animaux même; il devra faire sentir, palper, écouter ses inventions; si ce qu'il rapporte *de là-bas* a forme, il donne forme: si c'est informe, il donne de l'informe. Trouver une langue.

> He is responsible for humanity, even for the animals; he will have to have his own inventions smelt, felt, and heard; if what he brings back *from down there* has form, he delivers form; if it is *informe*, he delivers *informe*. A language must be found.

"Informe" is often translated as "shapelessness" or "formlessness," which certainly isn't incorrect. But there's a problem with this translation since "informe" itself doesn't suggest an *absence* of form, but a notion of form that has *positive* qualities—it is the form of formlessness, not formlessness itself. I was inspired to make this decision because of a line that has always nagged me, again from Eliot's "Reflections on *Vers Libre*": "If *vers libre* is a genuine verse-form it will have a positive definition. And I can define it only in negatives: (1) absence of pattern, (2) absence of rhyme, (3) absence of metre." This line of argumentation (which I think Eliot was providing in a somewhat facetious, or even insincere, mood) sheds light on what Rimbaud might have meant here. After all, Rimbaud elsewhere in the letter argues for new *forms* of poetry by women—"man—until now abominable—having given her her release"—not to mention argues that the poet will be responsible "even for the *animals*." Directly after stating that the poet must "deliver" (my preference over the more literal translation "give") these *informe* poems, he writes: "A language must be found."

Translating *informe* as "shapelessness" seems to suggest that, adhering to an Aristotelian concept of hylomporphism, there could be poems—or sludge, or a collapsed building, or a decaying body—without any discernible "form" at all, and yet, we can agree that, witnessing any of these, one is confronted with something like form, even if these objects point to prior, more familiar or convenient, shapes.

The French philosopher and novelist Georges Bataille, who once declared that Baudelaire and Rimbaud were the only poets he could read without vomiting, wrote of the word "informe":

> A dictionary begins when it no longer gives the meaning of words, but their tasks. Thus formless [*informe*] is not only an adjective having a given meaning, but a term that serves to bring things down in the world, generally requiring that each thing have its form [*forme*]. What it designates has no rights in any sense and gets itself squashed everywhere, like a spider or an earthworm. In fact, for academic men to be happy, the universe would have to take shape [*forme*]. All of philosophy has no other goal: it is a matter of giving a frock coat to what is, a mathematical frock coat. On

the other hand, affirming that the universe resembles nothing and is only formless [*informe*] amounts to saying that the universe is something like a spider or spit.[*]

Bataille's general argument is that the universe *is*—there is an unordered movement among its elements, an immanent *becoming*—that it is always in *excess* of what the philosophers with their "mathematical frock coats" are willing to account for. Carried into Rimbaud's practice, one would never argue that the *Illuminations* are not poems due to a *lack* of form—they have the form they had when the poet, in Rimbaud's narrative from the letters, retrieved them from "*down there.*"

Yve-Alain Bois said of the word "informe," in an interview with *Artforum* concerning an exhibition he co-curated titled "L'Informe" inspired by Bataille's writing: "The word's untranslatable, but you can find approximations: formless or formlessness. But it's not a concept. [I]t's an anticoncept. [...] In Bataille's project... the *informe* is something like a first principle that defines what is excluded from Western metaphysics. The *informe* is understood as something that's going to *undo* categories." To this degree, I'd like this word to continue to trouble readers in English much as it troubles readers of the French. I chose to preserve the word in its original French, much as I did the word *dada* ("hobbyhorse") in "The Dazzling Victory of Sarrebruck"—you have now learned two French words.

The Organization of This Book

Rimbaud never had a chance to organize his verse poems in the way, for example, Baudelaire carefully did in *Les fleurs de mal* ("The Flowers of Evil")—that is, to group together those that had a thematic affinity. Rimbaud's poems represent, individually, singular *interventions*, which is to say, he rarely hit the same note twice, or reframed an old theme in a modestly novel way, so his poems seem to jar with each other, to struggle for

---

* *Visions of Excess. Selected Writings, 1927-1939*. Minneapolis: University of Minnesota Press, 1985.

attention, and never settle into a whole. Rimbaud once ordered his friend Paul Demeny to destroy all of his earlier poems, suggesting that he cared about the *body* of his work in the way most poets do. He had occasionally sketched tables of contents for proposed volumes prior to his life in Paris, but never made an attempt to have a book published outside of *Une saison en enfer*. Happily, Demeny did not follow through with the poet's directive. My basic organizational principle was to put the poems in chronological order of composition, as far as scholars are able to determine, within their individual sections. I've made a few exceptions to this rule, which I mention in the notes.

"Early Spring" begins with a Latin poem starting "Ver erat..." that Rimbaud wrote in three hours as a school assignment two weeks after he had turned fourteen. The task was to write a poem based on specific lines from Horace's *Odes*. The earliest poem that we have from Rimbaud, it's already characteristic of his later style, being largely a vision of his own confirmation as a poet: "Tu vates eres"—"you will be a poet"—or variously, a *prophet*. "Vates" is considered by scholars a loanword from the Celtic and is often translated as "bard" or "seer"; the more commonplace Latin word "poeta" could have sufficed for "poet."

Rimbaud's earliest known French poem, "The Orphans' New Year's Gifts," appears to be derived from another of Rimbaud's Latin compositions, written about the same time, which starts "Jamque novus..." and depicts a young child, seemingly orphaned in his own home, being visited by an angel. Later poems in this section have the poet imagining himself as something of the adolescent rake, the seducer, and decidedly heterosexual. These poems are probably the least celebrated among Rimbaud's readers in English as they lack the caustic satire, or the visionary expansiveness, or the confessional tone verging on abjection, of his later work. Some even dismiss them as exercises or imitations, though Ezra Pound included the entirety of "The First Evening" (which was then known by the title "Comédie en trois baisers," "Comedy in Three Kisses") in his essay "A Study of Modern French Poets" in 1918. The shortest of this set, "Sensation," in which the poet imagines himself as the "bohemian" voyager, anticipates his life and writing to come.

"First Marches" starts with "The Seekers of Lice" which, according to biographers, reflects the ministrations of his friend Georges Izambard's "aunts"—Izambard was an orphan who was raised by two sisters—during one of Rimbaud's long peregrinations through the French countryside. This section contains Rimbaud's first political poem, written while in Mazas Prison after having travelled by train to Paris without a ticket. "The Dazzling Victory of Sarrebruck" (which anticipates the movie *M.A.S.H.* by almost a century), "The Sleeper in the Valley" and "Evil" provide a rich portrait of the travesties of the Franco-Prussian war that Rimbaud witnessed traipsing through the countryside. These types of poems—editorial, engaged, and enraged—are exactly those that readers of Rimbaud who focus only on the visionary epiphanies of "Vowels" or the *Illuminations* tend to overlook.

"First Marches" also contains some of Rimbaud's most notable sonnets. "Venus Anadyomene" is a virulent attack on conventions of female "beauty" among the male academic and Parnassian artists and poets of this period, many of whose works concerning female perfection were devoted to prostitutes. The poem stands out as the first note of the violent *renunciation* of aesthetic standards, even of his own, that he would sound later with his writing about "implanting and cultivating warts on his face" in his "seer" letters and in *Une saison en enfer*. Equally startling, if for entirely different reasons, is "The Sideboard," a painterly study of an inanimate object which recalls his lines about the magical armoire in his earlier poem "The Orphans' New Year's Gifts." "First Marches" closes with three electric sonnets that fill out the portrait of Rimbaud as the paradigmatic "bohemian" —authentic products of the "orphan" vagabond that, to my mind, anticipate Frank O'Hara's city-walking poems with their excited cataloguing of experiences.

Rimbaud wrote remarkably few of his early major poems while living in Paris. His first experience of the city was the week he spent in prison during which he wrote a sonnet; little is known of what he did during the two weeks he spent there in March 1871. "The Drunken Boat," for example, was one of the poems Rimbaud arrived with when he first visited Verlaine in late September, 1871. I titled this next section "Approaching Paris" since, in this period of his life, "Paris," which was boiling with the activities of the Paris Commune, was most likely largely drawn from Rimbaud's readings in novels, history and the newspapers.

"Dance of the Hanged Men " is, quite literally, an example of Rimbaud's brand of "gallows humor." Here, he is not just laughing but confronting one of the major themes of his work—what, exactly, constitutes *courage*, and what disasters await someone devotedly, perhaps naively, dedicated to a heroic cause. "The Blacksmith," his longest work in couplets, is a compelling historical recreation based on an anecdote from the Insurrection of August 10, 1792 during the French Revolution when armed insurgents stormed the Tuileries Palace. The poem is in a late French Romantic style, and is only marked by Rimbaud's irony in the words of the Blacksmith himself—Rimbaud imagining himself as an enlightened *laborer*.

"The Customs Men" marks a change in Rimbaud's depiction of the itinerant life from the sonnets of the prior section as it narrates the humiliations he and others, young and old, encountered at the hands of corrupt, seedy customs officials while vagabonding. "Parisian War Song" is the first of the poems that Rimbaud included in his famous letter to Paul Demeny outlining his ideas concerning the "seer," and yet is replete with imagery of the Paris Commune that he would have received through the papers. "Parisian Orgy, or Paris is Repopulated," an extended apostrophe to a city depicted by turns as in ruins and utterly decadent, or ascendent and unrivaled in holiness, is almost indescribable as it flips, line by line, between insult and homage.

"Heresies" opens with "Tartuffe's Punishment," a sonnet which, with its tale of highway banditry, could have belonged among his bohemian poems, though in this case the victim is the pious Tartufe from Molière's play— one suspects that the bandit is Rimbaud himself. "Squattings" might be the most detailed consideration of a clergyman taking a shit in all of literature, while "The Poor in Church," caustic as it is, conveys a sympathy for unwitting Christian believers that he expressed in the earlier sonnet "Evil" but mixed with the extended satire of "Set to Music." "First Communions," written around the time his sister Isabelle received her first communion, is his most direct confrontation with the spiritual hypocrisies of the Church. The poem is a narrative, but unlike "The Orphans' New Year's Gifts" and "The Blacksmith," it is a collection of scenes or vignettes, voices and perspectives ever-shifting, that culminates in a scathing monologue by the victim, a young girl whose erotic energies had been coopted by the Church in an attempt to make her something like Jesus's spiritual lover. "Seven Year Old Poets" is a curio in that we have a seventeen-or-so year-old poet reflecting on his follies *as a youth* of seven, a singularly Rimbaudian brand of nostalgia. "The Sitting Men" is an imagistic decimation of the tired old men he encountered in Charleville's library while he was trying to coax the librarian into permitting him to read then-controversial books (Victor Hugo's novels, for example, or works about alchemy).

"The Seer" might be the most exciting section for fans of Rimbaud's two famous "Letters of the Seer" and the later prose poems such as *Illuminations*. The section starts with the lyric "The Stolen Heart," an account of a humiliating experience Rimbaud suffered at the hands either of common soldiers or of the Paris Communards themselves. He clearly saw this poem as a turning point in his writing as there are three versions of it, two of which were preserved in letters to his friends. The sonnet "Vowels," which attributes colors to each of the vowels, is so well-known that its very structure, not to mention its content, has become the subject of homage and, at times, parody. Much ink has been spilled in discerning the meaning of this poem, searching for a *code*, an alchemic matrix, that would illuminate why A is black, E is white, and so forth. If anything, the poem seems to express Rimbaud's belief in the aesthetic possibilities of *synaesthesia*, a neurological trait or condition in which the stimulation of one sense, say vision, triggers a sensation in another sense, say that of smell. In this case, a single letter, a black glyph, triggers the experience of a color.

"The Drunken Boat" has been hugely influential—it's impossible to imagine much of Surrealism, or Ginsberg's "Howl," or Bob Dylan's "It's Alright, Ma (I'm Only Bleeding)," without this example of the poet witnessing the "birth of his thought" in a myriad of sensations and associations verging on chaos. The entire "psychedelic" movement of the '60s seems to owe a debt to this poem.

"What Is Said to the Poet Concerning Flowers" is a withering, florid—it literally *withers* flowers—attack on the poet he most wanted to impress as a relative youth, Théodore de Banville. Cheekily, he sent this poem to Banville asking if he'd *improved* and signed the poem "Alcide Bava." "What is Said to the Poet" cycles through a catalogue of clichés he saw in the Parnassians, but also argues that a poet's attentions to flora and fauna and to exotic, distant landscapes should be with a scientific eye, maybe toward commercial exploitation. While Rimbaud's exact intentions in this poem, outside of his attack on the Parnassians, are difficult to pin down, it surely acts as a gloss on Rimbaud's later thinking on labor, science, duty and knowledge in *Une saison en enfer*, and which manifested in his subsequent career as a trader and geographer in Africa.

"The Album Zutique" was a collaborative notebook authored by Rimbaud and several of his friends, to the degree he had them, during their raucous gatherings in the Hôtel des Étrangers in Paris from September to October 1871 just months after the violent suppression of the Commune. The "Zutistes" adopted their name from the common word "zut" which, at the time, had a more potent connotation, as opposed to today where "zut" can be translated variously as "damn" or even "heck." The "Zutistes," with their commitment to the *negation* of contemporary artistic values, are often regarded as the the first truly avant-garde artist faction, anticipating the anti-art ethos of the Dada gatherings at the Cabaret Voltaire in 1916. The contents of the volume were largely parodic. A prime target was the then-ascendant poet François Coppée, known for his celebration of common lives and objects—"le poète des humbles," as he was known.

Most of Rimbaud's contributions were travesties of Coppée, though many—like the infamous "L'Idole. Sonnet du trou du cul" ("Idol. Sonnet to the Asshole"), co-written with Verlaine—parodied other poets, in this case the Parnassian Albert Mérat, the one who refused to sit for the group portrait "Un coin de table." Mérat had published a book of sonnets called *L'Idole* in which each poem extolled a body part of his mistress—with one notable omission. "Sonnet to the Asshole" can be seen as a sequel to Rimbaud's earliest attack on Parnassian notions of feminine beauty, "Venus Anadyomene," while at the same time celebrating homosexual love.

"Memories of an Old Moron," like "Seven Year Old Poets," offers a window on Rimbaud's sexuality when he was still a child, though in fact he wouldn't have had many opportunities to spend time with his father who, a journeyman soldier, only visited the family once a year to spawn a new child— Rimbaud had four siblings, one of whom died soon after birth—and never returned after Rimbaud's sixth year. This section closes with a few poems that weren't actually in the "Album Zutique," but which were in that spirit. Of special interest is "Saturnian Hypotyposes, From Belmontet," which, to my mind, parodies, as if in *anticipation*, the later style of Mallarmé (whom Rimbaud might have met), foreshadowing some of the themes and methods Mallarmé would employ in "Un coup de dés" ("A Throw of the Dice").

The next section title, "After the Rains," echoes what is often placed as the first poem of the *Illuminations* (which starts "After the flood had subsided..."). This section is the most chronologically coherent as most of the dates of composition are known. Many of these poems were written at the same time as, or soon after, those from the "Album Zutique" yet couldn't be more different. These poems hint at a resignation, a retreat from the fervor of the poems of the era of the Paris Commune and his "seer" period. "Comedy of Thirst," for example, quite explicitly marks a rejection of any recourse to drugs or alcohol to induce his visions, while "Good Thought in the Morning," "The Cassis River," "Tear," and "The Crows" are landscapes, anticipating the manner of the later Symbolist school of French poetry. Truly "objective," these poems are only modestly expressionistic, containing little of self-portraiture.

This section is particularly interesting for the light it sheds on the prose poems of the *Illuminations*. Rimbaud moves far afield of any classic French meters, those associated with the noblest forms of expression. While some of the poems deftly reshuffle metrical figures, their models are from the song and light verse that Rimbaud was enjoying at the time. "Amaranth flowerbeds...", "Hear how it knells..." and "Shame" are written with a looseness that wouldn't be out of place in 20th-century Anglophone free verse poetry. Rimbaud's eventual formal experiments in the *Illuminations* would be far more radical, but nonetheless, here we see the first definite stirrings of Rimbaud's desire to break free of fixed meter. In "Amaranth flowerbeds..." Rimbaud strays into a level of indeterminacy that is only rivaled by his later prose poems—indeed, this poem could be considered the first *Illumination*.

The one poem in this section that runs against this grain is his celebrated "Memory." Like "Ophelia" and other early works, the poem is written in alexandrines, ordered in rhyming quatrains, though with an extraordinarily knotty syntax that is new. The poem is often read as autobiographical; section III, in particular, seems to be a reflection upon his stern, uncompromising mother and his abandonment by his father. Several poems in "After the Rains" reappear, slightly revised, in *Une saison en enfer*, notably "The wolf cried...," "Eternity" and "Oh seasons, oh castles..."

The final section, "Fragments and Doggerel," contains occasional poems often written with, or to, friends. "Toilet Stall Verse" is two short poems that Verlaine remembers Rimbaud having written on a wall somewhere in Paris which Rimbaud signed "Albert Mérat." Verlaine used the single line, "It rains softly," at the head of his poem "Il pleure dans mon coeur" but it seems the poem itself has been lost. I placed another fragment of a poem, "The Just Man," in the "Heresies" section of this book since it is substantial and is his most potent attack on bourgeois notions of morality. But I put "You have lied...," another fragment, in this last section merely to be a completist as it's not much more than a badly-drawn cartoon.

The one poem we have of Rimbaud after his renunciation of verse around 1872 is the squib "One gets hungry in this old barracks room..." which he included in a letter to Ernest Delahaye in 1875. André Breton, leader of the Surrealists, saw this poem as "the absolute triumph of pantheistic delirium." Others don't consider it a poem at all. I gave it its own section since it was written so long after he had apparently abandoned verse and because I quite like my rendition of it.

I should mention that the title of this volume is actually from Wallace Fowlie's 1966 edition of his translations of Rimbaud in which he titled a sequence "Festivals of Patience." This sequence is now known as "Patience"; most likely, Fowlie had just followed whatever was current in the French editions he was basing his translations on. But this oxymoronic phrase, "festivals of patience," has circulated in my head since my high school days when I'd first read Fowlie's collection, even as I've never quite known what it meant—so I decided to use it.

In Closing

I had a difficult time writing this introduction. I felt that anything I would want to say about Rimbaud's poetry was in the translations themselves. I wanted to write a few notes on my method, aimed primarily at those who either knew the poems in their original French, through other translations, or who have an interest in the process of translation itself. Naturally, I also wanted to give to the general reader coming across this poetry for the first time some context, but I didn't want to stray too deeply into Rimbaud's life—which was so remarkable that a feature film, *Total Eclipse* (1995), starring Leonardo DiCaprio as Rimbaud, was based on it (David Thewlis played Verlaine)—or into the countless cultural figures who have been impacted by his work. I certainly didn't want to write anything autobiographical.

I asked Jennifer Moxley, a great poet and longtime friend, to write a brief forward. She had already given me some great notes about the translations, and was enthusiastic about the book as a whole. In her forward, she managed to write everything I was fretting about writing in the most elegant, concise manner. She managed to encapsulate in one or two fluent sentences sentiments I might have wanted to write—for instance, the impact of Rimbaud on one's high school life as a novice poet and closet, inarticulate rebel—in a witty, attractive way, and not the least poisoned by an academic tone or perspective. I can't thank her enough.

I also want to thank the scholar and poet Jeremy Schmidt who, as my freelance editor, offered great comments on drafts of this introduction. Jeremy (and Jennifer, voluntarily) also helped me clean up my grammar, my typos, my bad jokes, my oversights, my convoluted phrasings, my self-criticism and so forth. Of course, I want to thank another friend, the editor and publisher of Kenning Editions, Patrick Durgin. He's been a great collaborator on this project ever since he agreed to publish the book, and is a model of patience. Lastly, I'd like to thank Faride Mereb who designed the great cover of the book. I had asked that the famous photo by Carjat of Rimbaud not appear on the cover since I feel it's been a little over-exposed, and she came up with a wonderful compromise.

I'm dedicating the translation "Ophelia" to my friend Pegah Savehshemshaki, the "predator posing as a house pet," who was my most devoted follower on Facebook as I posted (and quickly deleted) these translations as they were written.

The book in its entirety is dedicated to my late friend, the poet Michael O'Brien, the first poet I had ever met, and who I, snottily, rarely listened to as a young upstart in Rutherford, New Jersey—he kept crossing out words in poems I had *spent months on*, and he really had no patience for avant-garde pretensions or the New York School—but who I admired and grew to love greatly. He taught me quite a bit about "America"—he was from Illinois, which naturally made him an authority—which was valuable for a half-Korean kid who most people in my nearly-all-white suburb, the Vietnam War still raging, didn't consider American at all. He was one of my mother's best friends and, along with his wife, Moira, took care of her, and by extension our whole family, when times were rough. He probably didn't die a saint either, but he was true.

1: EARLY SPRING

[A]nd so I have begun, only a child, but touched by the finger of the Muse (excuse me if this is banal) to write down my dear beliefs, my hopes, my sensations, all the things that poets do—this is what I call spring.

—Rimbaud to To Théodore de Banville, May 24, 24, 1870

"It Was Spring"

It was spring. An ailment kept Orbilius in
Rome, crippled. My barbarous teacher's tactics were
dispelled—the sounds of his blows now distant echoes.
My arms were nearly restored from his lashing rod.
I seized the chance: I mounted the beckoning hills,
left behind all memories. Free from cares, far from
my studies, easy joys cured my wasted spirit.
I don't know what charm it was that freed my heart and
dispelled the tedium my teacher's voice instilled—
I reveled in contemplating the vast landscape,
the happy miracles of the earth in mid-spring.
My boy's heart sought more than vain rambles over the
countryside—it reached for higher aspirations!
A divine mind somehow granted to me these wings.
Struck with a stupor, I stayed there, silent, my eyes
lost in contemplation. I sensed, warm within me,
a pure love for nature rise, like a ring of iron
moves with a secret force to a magnesium stone
and binds to it, quietly, with invisible hooks.

Nevertheless, resting my limbs exhausted by
my long rambles, I lay by the river's verdure.
The water's shy murmurs lulled me to sleep. I stretched
this time in the wind's breath for as long as I could.
Then, through the airy valley, a bustle of doves
floated, a white troop, bearing in their beaks wreathes of
scented blooms that Venus had gathered in Cyprus.
Their swarm flew gently over the grass where I lay.
Softly beating their wings, hovering above me
they ringed my head and bound my hands with a leafy
chain; crowning my temples with a fragrant myrtle
they bore me, like a toy, into the vacant air...
The flock raised me up to the high clouds half dozing
under a bower of roses. The wind caressed

my gently swinging bed with its breath. Once the doves
returned to their native haunts, and dizzyingly
had attained their hanging sanctuaries, they dropped
me down, now awake, and abandoned me quickly.
Oh, the sweet nests of birds! A pure white light shimmered
around my shoulders, friendly with its clinging beams.
This was not the light one encounters in daytime,
that light thick, shadowy, that obscures our vision.
This was a light not of earth—a celestial light!
This otherworldliness saturated my breast
completely, I know not how, like a howling flood.

Eventually, the birds returned, bearing in
their beaks a crown of laurels woven like the one
Apollo wears when plucking his melodic strings.
But when I was crowed with these laurels, the heavens
ripped opened above me—awestruck, I suddenly
saw Phoebus flying above the gold clouds. He gave
me with his divine hands a sonorous plectrum.
Then, he wrote upon my head with letters of fire:
"YOU WILL BE A POET." An incredible heat
flowed through all my limbs, a limpid fountain lit up
like a sheet of pure crystal by the sunlight's rays.
The doves themselves metamorphosed from their own forms;
a choir of Muses came, singing with soft voices
their sweet hymns. They lifted me as they repeated
thrice their omen—and thrice crowning me with laurel!

NOVEMBER 6, 1868
WRITTEN IN THREE HOURS FOR LATIN EXAMINATION

Les etrennes des orphelins

I.

La chambre est pleine d'ombre; on entend vaguement
De deux enfants le triste et doux chuchotement.
Leur front se penche, encore alourdi par le rêve,
Sous le long rideau blanc qui tremble et se soulève...
—Au dehors les oiseaux se rapprochent frileux;
Leur aile s'engourdit sous le ton gris des cieux;
Et la nouvelle Année, à la suite brumeuse,
Laissant traîner les plis de sa robe neigeuse,
Sourit avec des pleurs, et chante en grelottant...

II.

Or les petits enfants, sous le rideau flottant,
Parlent bas comme on fait dans une nuit obscure.
Ils écoutent, pensifs, comme un lointain murmure...
Ils tressaillent souvent à la claire voix d'or
Du timbre matinal, qui frappe et frappe encor
Son refrain métallique en son globe de verre...
—Puis, la chambre est glacée... on voit traîner à terre
Épars autour des lits, des vêtements de deuil:
L'âpre bise d'hiver qui se lamente au seuil
Souffle dans le logis son haleine morose!
On sent, dans tout cela, qu'il manque quelque chose...
—Il n'est donc point de mère à ces petits enfants,
De mère au frais sourire, aux regards triomphants?
Elle a donc oublié, le soir seule et penchée,
D'exciter une flamme à la cendre arrachée,
D'amonceler sur eux la laine et l'édredon
Avant de les quitter en leur criant: pardon.
Elle n'a point prévu la froideur matinale,
Ni bien fermé le seuil à la bise hivernale?...
—Le rêve maternel, c'est le tiède tapis,
C'est le nid cotonneux où les enfants tapis,
Comme de beaux oiseaux que balancent les branches,

The Orphans' New Year's Gifts

I.

The room dances with shadows; the sad, soft whispers
of two children, indistinct, halting, can be heard.
Their heads decline heavily, still weighted with dreams
under the long white bed curtains that drift and breathe...
—Outside, birds nestle cosily against the cold;
their wings grow numb beneath a gray awning of clouds;
and the New Year, dragging her long raiment of fog,
walks the street stiffly, adjusting her snowy smock,
smiles through her tears and, though shivering, she sings...

II.

But the small children, under the curtain's swaying,
speak as if hiding, as one does on a dark night,
listening, as if to distant murmurs, eyes wide...
Often, they are shaken by the pure golden voice
of the morning bell that rings, again, its proud noise,
a metallic refrain sung within its glass sphere
—Then, the room is icy; one sees spread on the floor
bunched up around the bed... the children's mourning clothes.
The bitter wind of winter moans outside the door
and blows into the house with its somber rasping!
One senses, in this scene, that there's something missing...
—Where is the mother of these small, frightened children,
the mother with her fresh smile, with triumphant glances?
Ah, that night she forgot, alone and leaning down,
to sift through the ashes for some kindling to burn,
to pile high upon them their quilts, wools and sheets,
calling back, as she left them: Children, forgive me!
Shouldn't she have foreseen this cold winter morning?
Didn't she shut the door against the wind's thrashing?
—The perfect maternal dream is a warm blanket,
a nest of down where snuggles her little children
like pretty birds rocked in a tree's swaying branches

Dorment leur doux sommeil plein de visions blanches!...
—Et là,—c'est comme un nid sans plumes, sans chaleur
Où les petits ont froid, ne dorment pas, ont peur;
Un nid que doit avoir glacé la bise amère...

III.

Votre cœur l'a compris:—ces enfants sont sans mère.
Plus de mère au logis!—et le père est bien loin!...
—Une vieille servante, alors, en a pris soin.
Les petits sont tout seuls en la maison glacée;
Orphelins de quatre ans, voilà qu'en leur pensée
S'éveille, par degrés, un souvenir riant...
C'est comme un chapelet qu'on égrène en priant:
—Ah! quel beau matin, que ce matin des étrennes!
Chacun, pendant la nuit, avait rêvé des siennes
Dans quelque songe étrange où l'on voyait joujoux,
Bonbons habillés d'or, étincelants bijoux,
Tourbillonner, danser une danse sonore,
Puis fuir sous les rideaux, puis reparaître encore!
On s'éveillait matin, on se levait joyeux,
La lèvre affriandée, en se frottant les yeux...
On allait, les cheveux emmêlés sur la tête,
Les yeux tout rayonnants, comme aux grands jours de fête,
Et les petits pieds nus effleurant le plancher
Aux portes des parents tout doucement toucher...
On entrait!... Puis alors les souhaits... en chemise,
Les baisers répétés, et la gaîté permise.

IV.

Ah! c'était si charmant, ces mots dits tant de fois!
—Mais comme il est changé, le logis d'autrefois:
Un grand feu pétillait, clair, dans la cheminée,
Toute la vieille chambre était illuminée;
Et les reflets vermeils, sortis du grand foyer,
Sur les meubles vernis aimaient à tournoyer...
—L'armoire était sans clefs!... sans clefs, la grande armoire!
On regardait souvent sa porte brune et noire...

sleeping their sweet sleep full of white, soothing visions!
—But here: it's like a featherless nest, very cold,
where the children never sleep, so scared, so alone;
a nest the sour winter wind has frozen over...

III.

Your heart has discerned...—these children have no mother!
No mother in the home! the father far away!
—An old servant has seen, since, solely to their care,
the little ones alone in their iced-over house,
four-year-old orphans whose delicate thoughts are now
wakened, but slowly, by a smiling memory...
It is like a rosary you tell as you pray.
—Ah, what a beautiful dawn! this New Year's morning!
during the night, each one dreamt of one he's loving
in some strange dream where one sees amazing baubles,
candies dressed in gold, fine jewelry that sparkles,
galumphing around, dancing their sonorous dance,
and then, poof...—before staging a grand reentrance!
When you woke the next day, your heart was full of joy,
your mouth watering, and rubbing your sleepy eyes
you stumbled down the hallway, your hair unsown hay,
your eyes bright, expectant, like on a holiday,
your small bare feet just brushing against the tile floor,
approaching, then barely touching, your folks' closed door...
You entered!... received good wishes... in your clean PJs...
—Then, the flood of kisses!—and all gaiety unreined!

IV.

Ah! they were charming, those words so often said!
—But now it has all changed, that dwelling we once had:
a big clear fire crackled beneath the old chimney,
the living room aglow with the fire's noble gleam,
and reddish reflections strayed outward from the hearth
to dance wildly upon the varnished furniture...
—The cupboard had no keys... no keys, the grand cupboard!
You often stared for hours at its dark, imposing doors...

Sans clefs!... c'était étrange! . ., on rêvait bien des fois
Aux mystères dormant entre ses flancs de bois,
Et l'on croyait ouïr, au fond de la serrure
Béante, un bruit lointain, vague et joyeux murmure...
—La chambre des parents est bien vide, aujourd'hui:
Aucun reflet vermeil sous la porte n'a lui;
Il n'est point de parents, de foyer, de clefs prises:
Partant, point de baisers, point de douces surprises!
Oh! que le jour de l'an sera triste pour eux!
—Et, tout pensifs, tandis que de leurs grands yeux bleus
Silencieusement tombe une larme amère,
Ils murmurent: "Quand donc reviendra notre mère?"

V.

Maintenant, les petits sommeillent tristement:
Vous diriez, à les voir, qu'ils pleurent en dormant,
Tant leurs yeux sont gonflés et leur souffle pénible!
Les tout petits enfants ont le cœur si sensible!
—Mais l'ange des berceaux vient essuyer leurs yeux,
Et dans ce lourd sommeil met un rêve joyeux,
Un rêve si joyeux, que leur lèvre mi-close,
Souriante, semblait murmurer quelque chose...
—Ils rêvent que, penchés sur leur petit bras rond,
Doux geste du réveil, ils avancent le front,
Et leur vague regard tout autour d'eux se pose...
Ils se croient endormis dans un paradis rose...
Au foyer plein d'éclairs chante gaîment le feu...
Par la fenêtre on voit là-bas un beau ciel bleu;
La nature s'éveille et de rayons s'enivre...
La terre, demi-nue, heureuse de revivre,
A des frissons de joie aux baisers du soleil...
Et dans le vieux logis tout est tiède et vermeil:
Les sombres vêtements ne jonchent plus la terre,
La bise sous le seuil a fini par se taire...
On dirait qu'une fée a passé dans cela!...
—Les enfants, tout joyeux, ont jeté deux cris... Là,
Près du lit maternel, sous un beau rayon rose,

No keys!... how strange!... you would often hypothesize
of the mysteries that slept within its oak sides;
and from the depths of the keyhole's tunnel, you'd hear
a distant noise... a breath... a vague, joyful murmur...
—Today, the parents' room is entirely bare:
no more the red reflections that graced the door there,
no more the parents, nor the hearth, nor the stolen keys,
and therefore no more kisses, no sweet pleasantries!
Ah! how sad New Year's Day will be for these lost kids
—And, pensively, while from their fluttering eyelids
a silent bitter tear drops, like from the spring's first dew
—They purr together: "Oh, when will our mother return?"

V.

And now... the children sleep, only very sadly:
seeing them, you'd say they are crying in their sleep
so swollen their eyes, so pitifully they breathe!
Small children have souls that are sensitive, yet keen!
—But the Angels Who Watch Cradles wipe their eyes dry,
slip into their deep sleep a giddy lullaby,
a dream so happy, you hear from their half-closed lips
a soft murmuring, as they seem to smile a bit...
—They dream that, with the sweet motions of leaving bed,
leaning on their small arms, raising their fuzzy heads,
they scan the land around them, squinting their blue eyes...
What? have they been sleeping in a pink paradise
beside the bright hearth, where the fire gaily dances?
Through the window, azure skies paint the far distance;
Nature wakens, grows intoxicated with light...
the earth, half-bare, impatient to get on with its life,
stirs with joy, and receives its kisses from the sun...
and all the house is bathed in warm, reddish tones.
Their somber garb no longer sprawls across the floor,
the wind finally ceasing to pound the old door...
What? Has a fairy made a magic cameo?
The children, overjoyed, burst out with two shouts... Look!
near the mother's bed, lit up by rose-colored rays,

Là, sur le grand tapis, resplendit quelque chose...
Ce sont des médaillons argentés, noirs et blancs,
De la nacre et du jais aux reflets scintillants;
Des petits cadres noirs, des couronnes de verre,
Ayant trois mots gravés en or: "À NOTRE MERE!"

there, on the big rug, is something that scintillates...
A small host of silver medallions, black and white,
mother-of-pearl and dark jet, glittering with light,
small black frames, glass wreathes, gilt chalices and flowers,
and three words engraved in bright gold: "TO OUR MOTHER!"

1869/PUBLISHED JANUARY 2, 1870

Sensation

Par les soirs bleus d'été, j'irai dans les sentiers,
Picoté par les blés, fouler l'herbe menue:
Rêveur, j'en sentirai la fraîcheur à mes pieds.
Je laisserai le vent baigner ma tête nue.

Je ne parlerai pas, je ne penserai rien:
Mais l'amour infini me montera dans l'âme,
Et j'irai loin, bien loin, comme un bohémien,
Par la Nature—heureux comme avec une femme.

Mars 1870

Sensation

I'll stroll, through cool summer evenings, the country roads,
grass nipping my ankles, treading sprite-like through wheat;
I'll lie about, a-dream, as dew silvers my soles,
my long hair loosened—tossed by a soft August breeze.

I won't speak. I'll be mute. I will banish all thought.
I will wander miles like a true bohemian,
as infinite love surges and restricts my breath,
through calm pastures, joyful, as if with a woman.

MARCH, 1870

Soleil et chair [Credo in unam]

I.

Le Soleil, le foyer de tendresse et de vie,
Verse l'amour brûlant à la terre ravie,
Et, quand on est couché sur la vallée, on sent
Que la terre est nubile et déborde de sang;
Que son immense sein, soulevé par une âme,
Est d'amour comme dieu, de chair comme la femme,
Et qu'il renferme, gros de sève et de rayons,
Le grand fourmillement de tous les embryons!

Et tout croît, et tout monte!
                      —Ô Vénus, à Déesse!

Je regrette les temps de l'antique jeunesse,
Des satyres lascifs, des faunes animaux,
Dieux qui mordaient d'amour l'écorce des rameaux
Et dans les nénuphar baisaient la Nymphe blonde!
Je regrette les temps où la sève du monde,
L'eau du fleuve, le sang rose des arbres verts
Dans les veines de Pan mettaient un univers!
Où le sol palpitait, vert, sous ses pieds de chèvre;
Où, baisant mollement le clair syrinx, sa lèvre
Modulait sous le ciel le grand hymne d'amour;
Où, debout sur la plaine, il entendait autour
Répondre à son appel la Nature vivante;
Où les arbres muets, berçant l'oiseau qui chante,
La terre berçant l'homme, et tout l'Océan bleu
Et tous les animaux aimaient, aimaient en Dieu!

Je regrette les temps de la grande Cybèle
Qu'on disait parcourir gigantesquement belle,
Sur un grand char d'airain, les splendides cités;
Son double sein versait dans les immensités
Le pur ruissellement de la vie infinie.

Sun and Flesh [Credo in Unam]

I.

That hearth of tenderness and life, the sun
pours over earth, to its delight, boiling love
and, when you lie in the valley, you feel
that rich blood flows beneath, that the earth is nubile
and that, lifted by a soul, the earth's breast
is made of love, like God, and like woman, of flesh
and that, flowing with sap deep within, a light glows
stirring the vast swarming of all the embryos!

And all grows, all aspires!
                              —Oh Venus, oh goddess!

I miss the days of ancient youth: lascivious
satyrs, animal fauns, and all the Gods who gnawed,
in the madness of love, on a branch's soft bark,
and kissed the blonde Nymph, encircled by nénuphars!
I miss the time when the world's sap—the flows of the
river, the storms, the rosy blood of green
trees—infused with a vast universe old Pan's veins
and the earth trembled, green, beneath his goat feet
and his lips, softly kissing the Syrinx, set
sounding beneath the heavens the great hymn of love,
and when, on a plain, he heard his echo
about him—living Nature answering his call—
and the mute trees made with their branches a cradle
for the singing bird, the earth cradling man, the seas
and all beasts—and all, all loved in the Deity!

I long for the times of the great Cybele
who ventured, it is said, immensely beautiful
in a great bronze chariot through splendid cities;
her twin breasts poured into the profound, yawning deeps
its streams—tributaries of infinite life!

L'Homme suçait, heureux, sa mamelle bénie,
Comme un petit enfant, jouant sur ses genoux.
—Parce qu'il était fort, l'Homme était chaste et doux.

Misère! Maintenant il dit: Je sais les choses,
Et va, les yeux fermés et les oreilles closes.
—Et pourtant, plus de dieux! plus de dieux! L'Homme est Roi,
L'Homme est Dieu! Mais l'Amour voilà la grande Foi!
Oh! si l'homme puisait encore à ta mamelle,
Grande mère des dieux et des hommes, Cybèle;
S'il n'avait pas laissé l'immortelle Astarté
Qui jadis, émergeant dans l'immense clarté
Des flots bleus, fleur de chair que la vague parfume,
Montra son nombril rose où vint neiger l'écume,
Et fit chanter Déesse aux grands yeux noirs vainqueurs,
Le rossignol aux bois et l'amour dans les cœurs!

II.

Je crois en toi! je crois en toi! Divine mère,
Aphrodité marine!—Oh! la route est amère
Depuis que l'autre Dieu nous attelle à sa croix;
Chair, Marbre, Fleur Vénus, c'est en toi que je crois!
—Oui, l'Homme est triste et laid, triste sous le ciel vaste,
Il a des vêtements, parce qu'il n'est plus chaste,
Parce qu'il a sali son fier buste de dieu,
Et qu'il a rabougri, comme une idole au feu,
Son corps Olympien aux servitudes sales!
Oui, même après la mort, dans les squelettes pâles
Il veut vivre, insultant la première beauté!
—Et l'Idole où tu mis tant de virginité,
Où tu divinisas notre argile, la Femme,
Afin que l'Homme pût éclairer sa pauvre âme.
Et monter lentement, dans un immense amour
De la prison terrestre à la beauté du jour,
La Femme ne sait plus même être Courtisane!
—C'est une bonne farce! et le monde ricane
Au nom doux et sacré de la grande Venus!

Man suckled at her blesséd nipple in delight
playing like a little child at her knees
—and because he was strong, Man was gentle and chaste.

Oh horror! Now Man says: I know things—now he roams
around with his eyes tightly shut, and his ears closed.
—And yet, no more gods! no more gods! now Man is King,
Man is God! But Love is the supreme Conviction!
Oh! if only Man still drew strength from your nipple,
great nurturer of gods and men, Cybele,
if only he had not abandoned immortal
Astarte who, once, arising from a glowing squall
of blue waters, flower-flesh, perfumed by the waves,
disclosed her rosy navel where snowy foam raged
and—a goddess with defeating black eyes—made start
the nightingale's song in the woods—love in Man's heart!

II.

I believe! I believe in you, Divine Mother!
Sea-born Aphrodite! The path has been bitter
nailed to the one cross by the other God
—Flesh, Marble, Flower, Venus, I believe in you!
Yes, man is ugly, sad, beneath the sky so vast,
—ugly—because he is not chaste, he hides in rags,
because he has defiled his god-like, noble head,
and since, like an idol in the flames, he has bent
down his Olympian form to base slavery!
Yes, even after death, he insults pure beauty—
he wants to persist—as pale skeletons!
—And the Idol in whom you placed virginity,
in whom you made our clay divine, Woman,
so that Man might grace his soul with bright resplendence
and rise, in boundless love, from the earth's dull prison
toward the beauty of the day, toward azure heaven...
Woman lost the skill to be such a Courtesan!
A fine farce! And the world now busts a gut
at the sweet and sacred name of the great Venus!

III.

Si les temps revenaient, les temps qui sont venus!
—Car l'Homme a fini! l'Homme a joué tous les rôles!
Au grand jour, fatigué de briser des idoles
Il ressuscitera, libre de tous ses Dieux,
Et, comme il est du ciel, il scrutera les cieux!
L'Idéal, la pensée invincible, éternelle,
Tout le dieu qui vit, sous son argile charnelle,
Montera, montera, brûlera sous son front!
Et quand tu le verras sonder tout l'horizon,
Contempteur des vieux jougs, libre de toute crainte,
Tu viendras lui donner la Rédemption sainte!
—Splendide, radieuse, au sein des grandes mers
Tu surgiras, jetant sur le vaste Univers
L'Amour infini dans un infini sourire!
Le Monde vibrera comme une immense lyre
Dans le frémissement d'un immense baiser!

—Le Monde a soif d'amour: tu viendras l'apaiser.
. . . .

[Ô! L'Homme a relevé sa tête libre et fière!
Et le rayon soudain de la beauté première
Fait palpiter le dieu dans l'autel de la chair!
Heureux du bien présent, pâle du mal souffert,
L'Homme veut tout sonder,—et savoir! La Pensée,
La cavale longtemps, si longtemps oppressée
S'élance de son front! Elle saura Pourquoi!...
Qu'elle bondisse libre, et l'Homme aura la Foi!
—Pourquoi l'azur muet et l'espace insondable?
Pourquoi les astres d'or fourmillant comme un sable?
Si l'on montait toujours, que verrait-on là-haut?
Un Pasteur mène-t-il cet immense troupeau
De mondes cheminant dans l'horreur de l'espace?
Et tous ces mondes-là, que l'éther vaste embrasse,
Vibrent-ils aux accents d'une éternelle voix?

III.

If only those times that have passed might still grace us!
—For Man is done! He has exhausted all the roles!
At the height of noon, weary with smashing idols,
he will revive, and free from all his gods,
since he is born of heaven, he will scan the clouds!
The Ideal, that invincible, eternal thought,
the whole god who lives within his clay form,
will climb! will climb! and burn beneath his brow!
And, when you see him sounding the wide horizon,
disdainful of old yokes, free from inhibitions,
you will come and bequeath him—holy Redemption!
—Dazzling, radiant, from the womb of vast oceans,
you will rise, casting over the Cosmos,
infinite love—beaming through an infinite smile!
The World will vibrate, like an immense lyre
in the shuddering of an immense, boundless kiss.

—The World thirsts for love: you will come and quench its thirst.
. . . .

[Oh! Man has lifted his head, proud and free,
in a quick flash of primordial beauty, he
makes the god tremble at the altar of his flesh!
Now, happy in the good, pale from the ills he's felt,
Man aims to sound all the depths—and to know all! Thought,
a jade for so long, and for ages kept below,
erupts from his brow! And so, someday, she will know
the Why! Man would have Faith if he would let her soar!
—Why the silent sky, the unfathomable space?
Why the golden stars that swarm like glittering grains?
If one could climb forever, what would one see there?
Is this vast flock of worlds driven by a shepherd
on its journey through the horror of space?
Do these worlds that recline in the ether's embrace
tremble at the sentence of an eternal voice?

—Et l'Homme, peut-il voir? peut-il dire: je crois?
La voix de la pensée est-elle plus qu'un rêve?
Si l'homme naît si tôt, si la vie est si brève,
D'où vient-il? Sombre-t-il dans l'Océan profond
Des Germes, des Foetus, des Embryons, au fond
De l'immense Creuset d'où la Mère-Nature
Le ressuscitera, vivante créature,
Pour aimer dans la rose, et croître dans les blés?...

Nous ne pouvons savoir!—Nous sommes accablés
D'un manteau d'ignorance et d'étroites chimères!
Singes d'hommes tombés de la vulve des mères,
Notre pâle raison nous cache l'infini!
Nous voulons regarder:—le Doute nous punit!
Le doute, morne oiseau, nous frappe de son aile...
—Et l'horizon s'enfuit d'une fuite éternelle!...
. . . .

Le grand ciel est ouvert! les mystères sont morts
Devant l'Homme, debout, qui croise ses bras forts
Dans l'immense splendeur de la riche nature!
Il chante... et le bois chante, et le fleuve murmure
Un chant plein de bonheur qui monte vers le jour!...
—C'est la Rédemption! c'est l'amour! c'est l'amour!...]
. . . .

IV.

Ô splendeur de la chair! ô splendeur idéale!
Ô renouveau d'amour, aurore triomphale
Où, courbant à leurs pieds les Dieux et les Héros,
Kallipige la blanche et le petit Éros
Effleureront, couverts de la neige des roses,
Les femmes et les fleurs sous leurs beaux pieds écloses!
—Ô grande Ariadné, qui jettes tes sanglots
Sur la rive, en voyant fuir là-bas sur les flots
Blanche sous le soleil, la voile de Thésée,
Ô douce vierge enfant qu'une nuit a brisée,

And Man—can he see? Can "I believe" be his choice?
Is the voice of thought nothing but a dream?
If Man is born so early, if life is so brief,
whence does he come? Does he sink into the Ocean
of germs, Fetuses and Embryos to the floor
of the giant Crucible where Mother Nature
will resuscitate him, make a living creature,
to rear him in the wheat and to love in the rose?

We can never know!—We are blind, held down
by cloaks of ignorance, narrowed by chimeras!
Apes of men, fallen from mothers' vulvas—
our feeble reason hides the infinite from us!
We wish to perceive, but Doubt harshly punishes!
Doubt, that foul bird, smashes us with its wing...
—The horizon flies off, eternally fleeing...

. . . .

The great sky lies open! The mysteries are dead
before Man, erect, arms over his chest
inside the vast splendor of abundant Nature!
He sings... the woods sing, the river murmurs
a song full of joy that climbs to the sky above...
—It is our Redemption! It is love! It is love!]

. . . .

IV.

Oh splendor of the flesh! Oh splendorous Ideal!
Oh triumphant dawn! Oh love in its renewal!
When white Callipyge and little Eros
—prostrate at their feet are the Gods and the Heroes—
covered with the snow of rose petals, will caress,
open fully at their feet, women and flowers!
—Oh great Ariadne, who pour out your sorrows
on the shore, you can see, out there on the ocean,
white under the sun, the tall sails of Theseus
—oh sweet virgin child whom a dark night has broken,

Tais-toi! Sur son char d'or brodé de noirs raisins,
Lysios, promené dans les champs Phrygiens
Par les tigres lascifs et les panthères rousses,
Le long des fleuves bleus rougit les sombres mousses.
Zeus, Taureau, sur son cou berce comme une enfant
Le corps nu d'Europé, qui jette son bras blanc
Au cou nerveux du Dieu frissonnant dans la vague,
Il tourne lentement vers elle son œil vague;
Elle, laisse traîner sa pâle joue en fleur
Au front de Zeus; ses yeux sont fermés; elle meurt
Dans un divin baiser, et le flot qui murmure
De son écume d'or fleurit sa chevelure.
—Entre le laurier-rose et le lotus jaseur
Glisse amoureusement le grand Cygne rêveur
Embrassant la Léda des blancheurs de son aile;
—Et tandis que Cypris passe, étrangement belle,
Et, cambrant les rondeurs splendides de ses reins,
Étale fièrement l'or de ses larges seins
Et son ventre neigeux brodé de mousse noire,
—Héraclès, le Dompteur qui, comme d'une gloire,
Fort, ceint son vaste corps de la peau du lion,
S'avance, front terrible et doux, à l'horizon!

Par la lune d'été vaguement éclairée,
Debout, nue, et rêvant dans sa pâleur dorée
Que tache le flot lourd de ses longs cheveux bleus,
Dans la clairière sombre où la mousse s'étoile,
La Dryade regarde au ciel silencieux...
—La blanche Séléné laisse flotter son voile,
Craintive, sur les pieds du bel Endymion,
Et lui jette un baiser dans un pâle rayon...
—La Source pleure au loin dans une longue extase...
C'est la Nymphe qui rêve, un coude sur son vase,
Au beau jeune homme blanc que son onde a pressé.
—Une brise d'amour dans la nuit a passé,
Et, dans les bois sacrés, dans l'horreur des grands arbres,
Majestueusement debout, les sombres Marbres,

hush! On his golden chariot stocked with black grapes
Lysios, who's drawn through the fields of Phrygia
by lascivious tigers and russet panthers,
reddens the dark mosses along the blue rivers.
—Zeus, the Bull, cradles on his neck like an infant
nude Europa, clinging with pallid hands
to the God's tense neck, trembling in the waves...
Slowly, he turns to her his dream-like eyes...
She lets her pale, blossomy cheek recline
on the brow of Zeus... Her eyes are closing... She dies
in a divine kiss, and the murmuring waters
strew the flowers of their golden foam on her hair.
—Between the oleander and the louche lotus,
the great dreaming Swan slips amorously; he holds
Leda enveloped in the whiteness of his wing...
—And while Cypris passes by, oddly alluring,
arching the great curves of her noble back,
and displays with pride her large breasts' golden expanse
and snowy belly adorned with black moss
—Hercules, the Tamer, as if with a nimbus,
girds his strong body with a lion's skin,
his brow awful yet sweet, stretched on the horizon!

Vaguely illuminated by the summer moon,
naked, dreaming in her gilded pallor,
streaked with the heavy wave of her long blue tresses,
in the shady glade with its celestial moss,
the Dryad, erect, gazes at the silent sky...
—White Selene lets her veil float, timidly,
over the feet of beautiful Endymion
and throws him a kiss, a pale beam of sun...
—The Spring weeps in the distance, a long ecstasy...
it is the Nymph, elbow on urn, who dreams
of the handsome white youth her wave caressed...
—During the night, a light wind of love passed
and in the sacred wood, its nightmare of great trees,
the somber Marbles, erect in their majesty,

Les Dieux, au front desquels le Bouvreuil fait son nid,
—Les Dieux écoutent l'Homme et le Monde infini!

Mai 70

the Gods, on whose brows the Bullfinch weaves its nest,
—The Gods listen to Man, and to the Universe!

MAY, 1870

Ophélie

I.

Sur l'onde calme et noire où dorment les étoiles
La blanche Ophélia flotte comme un grand lys,
Flotte très lentement, couchée en ses longs voiles...
—On entend dans les bois lointains des hallalis.

Voici plus de mille ans que la triste Ophélie
Passe, fantôme blanc, sur le long fleuve noir;
Voici plus de mille ans que sa douce folie
Murmure sa romance à la brise du soir.

Le vent baise ses seins et déploie en corolle
Ses grands voiles bercés mollement par les eaux;
Les saules frissonnants pleurent sur son épaule,
Sur son grand front rêveur s'inclinent les roseaux.

Les nénuphars froissés soupirent autour d'elle;
Elle éveille parfois, dans un aune qui dort,
Quelque nid, d'où s'échappe un petit frisson d'aile:
—Un chant mystérieux tombe des astres d'or.

II.

Ô pâle Ophélia! belle comme la neige!
Oui tu mourus, enfant, par un fleuve emporté!
—C'est que les vents tombant des grands monts de Norwège
T'avaient parlé tout bas de l'âpre liberté;

C'est qu'un souffle, tordant ta grande chevelure,
À ton esprit rêveur portait d'étranges bruits;
Que ton cœur écoutait le chant de la Nature
Dans les plaintes de l'arbre et les soupirs des nuits;

C'est que la voix des mers folles, immense râle,
Bisait ton sein d'enfant, trop humain et trop doux;

Ophelia

In that river where stars slumber on blackened waves
white Ophelia floats, a fine lily. Calming,
she floats quite slowly, enmeshed in her trailing veils...
—You hear, in the distant woods, the hunt resounding.

For a thousand years, the young, sad Ophelia
has flowed, a pale phantom, down the long black river;
yes, a thousand years, her bracing, pure mania
has hummed its dark fable of love's misadventure.

The wind kisses her breasts—it forms into a wreath
her great veils that, carefully, old waters endow;
stooping willows drop on her shoulders thick hot tears;
tall reeds slope over her dreaming, ennobled brow.

The bending nénuphars sigh around the maiden;
at times, she awakens—within a sleeping alder—
a nest from which emerges bright rustlings of wings.
—A mysterious song descends from the golden stars.

II.

Yes, you died, my child, borne off by the river's waves!
Oh, pale Ophelia! Beautiful as the snow!
—It was the storms that whistled from peaks in Norway
that plied you with liberty, its cold, bitter gall.

It was those gusts only, twisting your ranging hair,
that instilled a doubt into your highborn spirit;
it was your heart entranced by songs that Nature bore
in the pining of trees—orations of the night.

That crazed voice of the seas, that damning plebiscite,
battered your child's heart, too human, ill at ease;

C'est qu'un matin d'avril, un beau cavalier pâle,
Un pauvre fou, s'assit muet à tes genoux!

Ciel! Amour! Liberté! Quel rêve, à pauvre Folle!
Tu te fondais à lui comme une neige au feu:
Tes grandes visions étranglaient ta parole
—Et l'Infini terrible effara ton œil bleu!

III.

—Et le Poète dit qu'aux rayons des étoiles
Tu viens chercher, la nuit, les fleurs que tu cueillis,
Et qu'il a vu sur l'eau, couchée en ses longs voiles,
La blanche Ophélia flotter comme un grand lys.

it was that April morning when that fine pale knight
—really, a poor madman—sat, a mute, at your knees!

Paradise! Love! Freedom! What a dream, silly girl!
You fell into him like snow melts into a fire;
your amorous visions throttled all of your words
—an awesome infinity frightened your blue eyes!

III.

—Yes, the poet says that, beneath the stars' small rays,
you return every night to retrieve the blooms you sheared,
and that he saw there, entombed in her trailing veils,
white Ophelia floating, a fine white lily.

MAY 15, 1870

Premiere soirée

"—Elle était fort déshabillée
Et de grands arbres indiscrets
Aux vitres jetaient leur feuillée
Malinement, tout près, tout près.

Assise sur ma grande chaise,
Mi-nue, elle joignait les mains
Sur le plancher frissonnaient d'aise
Ses petits pieds si fins, si fins.

—Je regardai, couleur de cire,
Un petit rayon buissonnier
Papillonner dans son sourire
Et sur son sein,—mouche au rosier.

—Je baisai ses fines chevilles.
Elle eut un doux rire brutal
Qui s'égrenait en claires trilles,
Un joli rire de cristal.

Les petits pieds sous la chemise
Se sauvèrent: "Veux-tu finir!"
—La première audace permise,
Le rire feignait de punir!

—Pauvrets palpitants sous ma lèvre,
Je baisai doucement ses yeux:
—Elle jeta sa tête mièvre
En arrière: "Oh! c'est encor mieux!...

"Monsieur, j'ai deux mots à te dire..."
—Je lui jetai le reste au sein
Dans un baiser, qui la fit rire
D'un bon rire qui voulait bien...

The First Evening

"—She was coy, in dishabille,
and the curious, clever trees,
threw against the window panes,
nearer... nearer... indiscreet leaves.

Half-clothed, she twisted her curls...
Nested within my comfy chair,
her small feet danced... fair...so fair...
—gaily, they trembled on the floor.

I watched a small and nervous
ray of light the color of wax
flutter on her smile and breast...
Oh! it's a fly on a rose-bush!

I kissed her pretty ankles...
—Suddenly, she laughed, so tender...
it spread out in limpid trills,
her lovely, crystalline laughter.

Small toes escaped from under
her petticoat: "Oh... you must cease!"
—Her laughter sought to erase
this first step in our history!

Guileless eyes that I softly kissed,
poor things trembling at my lips...
Her sentimental head bucked
—"Ha, that was hardly a surprise!"

"Mister, I've two words to say..."
—What was left, I left on her breast
in a well-aimed kiss—she laughed,
signaling that she was careless...

—Elle était fort déshabillée
Et de grands arbres indiscrets
Aux vitres jetaient leur feuillée
Malinement, tout près, tout près.

.

—She was coy, in dishabille,
and the curious, clever trees,
threw against the window panes,
nearer... nearer... indiscreet leaves.

PUBLISHED AUGUST 13, 1870

Les reparties de nina

Lui.—Ta poitrine sur ma poitrine,
    Hein? nous irions,
Ayant de l'air plein la narine,
    Aux frais rayons

Du bon matin bleu, qui vous baigne
    Du vin de jour?...
Quand tout le bois frissonnant saigne
    Muet d'amour

De chaque branche, gouttes vertes,
    Des bourgeons clairs,
On sent dans les choses ouvertes
    Frémir des chairs:

Tu plongerais dans la luzerne
    Ton blanc peignoir,
Rosant à l'air ce bleu qui cerne
    Ton grand œil noir,

Amoureuse de la campagne,
    Semant partout,
Comme une mousse de champagne,
    Ton rire fou:

Riant à moi, brutal d'ivresse,
    Qui te prendrais.
Comme cela,—la belle tresse,
    Oh!—qui boirais

Ton goût de framboise et de fraise,
    Ô chair de fleur!
Riant au vent vif qui te baise
    Comme un voleur;

Nina's Replies

He: With your breast upon my breast,
    right? we will run,
our nostrils taking in the breeze
    in the cool sun

of the blue morning that bathes you
    with daylight wine,
the woods quivering, bleeding, mute
    with its desire.

On every green branch, droplets
    and pale buds rest,
and you feel, in these things opened,
    quivering flesh:

and you would drag your white gown through
    alfalfa, while
making rose the blue that halos
    your great black eyes;

in love with the country, insane
    you will scatter
like bubbles floating in champagne
    your mad laughter:

laughing at me—who, a bit buzzed,
    leaps to catch you
just like this—by a trailing tress!
    —I would consume

your tastes of raspberry and strawberry,
    oh, flower-flesh!
laughing as the wind, like a thief,
    nuzzles your breast,

Au rose églantier qui t'embête
    Aimablement:
Riant surtout, à folle tête,
    À ton amant!...

(Dix-sept ans! Tu seras heureuse!
    —Oh, les grands prés!
Le grand campagne amoureuse!
    —Dis, viens plus près!...)

—Ta poitrine sur ma poitrine,
    Mêlant nos voix,
Lents, nous gagnerions la ravine,
    Puis les grands bois!...

Puis, comme une petite morte,
    Le cœur pâmé,
Tu me dirais que je te porte,
    L'œil mi-fermé...

Je te porterais, palpitante,
    Dans le sentier:
L'oiseau filerait son andante:
    Au Noisetier...

Je te parlerais dans ta bouche:
    J'irais, pressant
Ton corps, comme une enfant qu'on couche,
    Ivre du sang

Qui coule, bleu, sous ta peau blanche
    Aux tons rosés:
Et te parlant la langue franche...
    Tiens!...—que tu sais...

Nos grands bois sentiraient la sève
    Et le soleil

at the wild rose that teases you
    at its pleasure,
more, directing its laughter to
    your dumb lover.

(Seventeen! you'll be delighted!
    —the great pastures!
—the grand, amorous countryside!
    —Psst... move closer...)

With your breast upon my breast,
    our voices meshed,
patiently, we'd reach the forest,
    the loud rushes,

then, like a little corpse—your heart
    swooning—you would
tell me to lift you in my arms,
    your eyes half-closed;

I would carry you down the lane,
    trembling, in fear,
as a bird warbled its andante:
    Au Noisetier...

I'd speak into your mouth, and press
    as if to bed
your child-like body to my chest,
    drunk with the blood

that flows blue under your white skin
    with rosy tints,
speaking to you with that frank slang
    —see!... you get it!

Our great woods would smell of honey
    and the sun's orb

Sablerait d'or fin leur grand rêve
    Vert et vermeil.

Le soir?... Nous reprendrons la route
    Blanche qui court
Flânant, comme un troupeau qui broute,
    Tout à l'entour

Les bons vergers à l'herbe bleue,
    Aux pommiers tors!
Comme on les sent toute une lieue
    Leurs parfums forts!

Nous regagnerons le village
    Au ciel mi-noir;
Et ça sentira le laitage
    Dans l'air du soir;

Ça sentira l'étable, pleine
    De fumiers chauds,
Pleine d'un lent rythme d'haleine,
    Et de grands dos

Blanchissant sous quelque lumière;
    Et, tout là-bas,
Une vache fientera, fière,
    À chaque pas...

—Les lunettes de la grand-mère
    Et son nez long
Dans son missel; le pot de bière
    Cerclé de plomb,

Moussant entre les larges pipes
    Qui, crânement,
Fument: les effroyables lippes
    Qui, tout fumant,

would dust the fine green and bronze dream
    with flakes of gold.

In the evening?... We'd walk white paths
    that meander
over, under, this way and that
    like a slow herd.

Oh, the ripe orchards, blue grass, trees
    bent with apples,
how you can smell, a mile away,
    their hearty scents!

When the sky is half dark, we'd come
    back to the town,
there'd be the smell of milking cows
    floating around,

it would smell of the stables, full
    of warm manure,
slow rhythms of breathing exhaled,
    great backs that curve,

whitening under some far light;
    see, over there,
a cow dunging as if with pride
    as it steps forth!

—Grandmother's spectacles, and her
    nose deep within
her dry missal; the jug of beer
    circled with tin

foaming among the big-bowled pipes
    proudly spewing,
—the appalling, low hanging lips
    which, still puffing

Happent le jambon aux fourchettes
    Tant, tant et plus:
Le feu qui claire les couchettes
    Et les bahuts.

Les fesses luisantes et grasses
    D'un gros enfant
Qui fourre, à genoux, dans les tasses,
    Son museau blanc

Frôlé par un mufle qui gronde
    D'un ton gentil,
Et pourlèche la face ronde
    Du cher petit...

(Noir, rogue, au bord de sa chaise,
    Affreux profil,
Une vieille devant la braise
    Qui fait du fil;)

Que de choses verrons-nous, chère,
    Dans ces taudis,
Quand la flamme illumine, claire,
    Les carreaux gris!...

—Puis, petite et toute nichée
    Dans les lilas
Noirs et frais: la vitre cachée,
    Qui rit là-bas...

Tu viendras, tu viendras, je t'aime!
    Ce sera beau.
Tu viendras, n'est-ce pas, et même...

Elle.—*Et mon bureau?*

snatch ham from forks—it's not enough,
    some more! some more!
the fire lighting up the bunks
    and the cupboards,

the glistening, fat buttocks of
    the big baby
who sticks his snout into the cups,
    still on his knees,

tickled gently by a doggie,
    growling nicely,
that licks the chubby cheeks of the
    precious darling...

(Near the embers, an old woman,
    black silhouette,
haughty, creepy, on her chair's edge,
    quietly knits...)

What sights we shall see, my bonbon,
    in these hovels,
when the fire sheds its light upon
    the gray windows!

And then, small, nestled in the cool
    of dark lilacs,
can you see?—a hidden window
    smiles in the dark...

You will come, you will come, my love!
    on this great lark!
you will come, no? yes?... in spite of...

She: *And blow off work?*

AUGUST 15, 1870

Les effarés

Á Monsieur Jean Aicard

Noirs dans la neige et dans la brume,
Au grand soupirail qui s'allume,
    Leurs culs en rond,

À genoux, cinq petits,—misère!
Regardent le Boulanger faire
    Le lourd pain blond...

Ils voient le fort bras blanc qui tourne
La pâte grise, et qui l'enfourne
    Dans un trou clair:

Ils écoutent le bon pain cuire.
Le boulanger au gras sourire
    Chante un vieil air.

Ils sont blottis, pas un ne bouge
Au souffle du soupirail rouge
    Chaud comme un sein.

Quand, pour quelque médianoche,
Plein de dorures de brioche
    On sort le pain,

Quand, sous les poutres enfumées
Chantent les croûtes parfumées
    Et les grillons;

Quand ce trou chaud souffle la vie;
Ils ont leur âme si ravie
    Sous leurs haillons,

The Astonished

To Monsieur Jean Aicard

Black in the snow and fog, they crowd
a flaming window grate, a round
    of close rear ends,

five children on their knees—so poor!
—they gaze on the working Baker,
    his golden bread.

They watch the strong white arms kneading
the gray dough—him sticking it
    in the bright hole.

They listen to the good bread cook.
The Baker, with a naive look,
    hums an old air.

They are quite packed in—not one moves
for, from the red window, the fumes
    warm like a breast.

And when—a middle-of-night nosh!—
plump and sweating like a brioche,
    arrives the bread—

when, beneath beams blackened with smoke,
the honey-smelling crust emotes,
    and the crickets—

when that warm hole exhales with life,
their young souls grow happy, delight
    in their garments.

Ils se ressentent si bien vivre,
Les pauvres petits pleins de givre,
    Qu'ils sont là, tous,

Collant leurs petits museaux roses
Au treillage, et disant des choses,
    Entre les trous,

Des chuchotements de prière;
Repliés vers cette lumière
    Du ciel rouvert

Si fort, qu'ils crèvent leur culotte
Et que leur lange blanc tremblote
    Au vent d'hiver.

They feel so renewed, so alive
these frost-covered, delicate tykes,
     that they could sing,

gluing their tiny pink noses
to the grate and stuffing the holes
     with muttered things

—quite silly! saying their prayers,
crouching before the light, near their
     revived heaven.

They crouch so hard, they tear their pants,
and now their undone shirts can dance
     in winter wind.

SEPTEMBER 20, 1870/REVISED JUNE, 1871

Roman

I.

On n'est pas sérieux, quand on a dix-sept ans.
—Un beau soir, foin des bocks et de la limonade,
Des cafés tapageurs aux lustres éclatants!
—On va sous les tilleuls verts de la promenade.

Les tilleuls sentent bon dans les bons soirs de juin!
L'air est parfois si doux, qu'on ferme la paupière;
Le vent chargé de bruits,—la ville n'est pas loin,—
A des parfums de vigne et des parfums de bière...

II.

—Voilà qu'on aperçoit un tout petit chiffon
D'azur sombre, encadré d'une petite branche,
Piqué d'une mauvaise étoile, qui se fond
Avec de doux frissons, petite et toute blanche...

Nuit de juin! Dix-sept ans!—On se laisse griser.
La sève est du champagne et vous monte à la tête...
On divague; on se sent aux lèvres un baiser
Qui palpite là, comme une petite bête...

III.

Le cœur fou Robinsonne à travers les romans,
—Lorsque, dans la clarté d'un pâle réverbère,
Passe une demoiselle aux petits airs charmants,
Sous l'ombre du faux-col effrayant de son père...

Et, comme elle vous trouve immensément naïf,
Tout en faisant trotter ses petites bottines,
Elle se tourne, alerte et d'un mouvement vif...
—Sur vos lèvres alors meurent les cavatines...

Novel

I.

We're all a sort of fool when we are seventeen.
One late evening—who cares for beer and lemonade!
the catty cafés, their flickering lamplit scenes!
—We'll wander as we will under green linden trees.

The lindens smell pure on these endless, pure June eves,
at times, the scents so strong, we must shutter our eyes.
The breeze is charged with sounds—the village is nearby—
and filled with odor of grape and odor of wine.

II.

—Look, you can see, look: a small blot of dark azure
framed by a hanging branch — it seems to dangle there,
pinned by a mischievous star who enjoys collage,
and who trembles, tiny and white, then disappears.

Oh, June night! Seventeen years old! We're overwhelmed.
The sap is champagne and it bubbles to our heads.
We talk like maniacs; a kiss makes itself known...
a kiss that lingers on the lips, a stunned insect.

III.

Our foolish hearts Crusoe across endless novels,
when, in the bright emissions of a pale streetlamp,
a beautiful girl walks by, charming, an eighth wonder,
though dragged in the wake of her dreadful father—trapped.

And, because she thinks you don't know very much, she
clicks her little boots, and fingers her loose bracelet,
and turns, abruptly, but nonetheless quite slyly
—the cavatinas fade with your faltering breath.

IV.

Vous êtes amoureux. Loué jusqu'au mois d'août.
Vous êtes amoureux.—Vos sonnets La font rire.
Tous vos amis s'en vont, vous êtes mauvais goût.
—Puis l'adorée, un soir, a daigné vous écrire...!

—Ce soir-là,...—vous rentrez aux cafés éclatants,
Vous demandez des bocks ou de la limonade...
—On n'est pas sérieux, quand on a dix-sept ans
Et qu'on a des tilleuls verts sur la promenade.

29 sept. 70

IV.

You are in love. You are loony until August.
You are in love. And your... your sonnets make her laugh!
Your friends get sick of you. You're becoming a putz.
—Then, one fine day, that one you worship demeans herself...

and writes! That very evening, you rejoin the scene,
cafés, chatter, beer and lemonade, naturally.
We're all a sort of fool when we are seventeen,
when we spend endless nights under green linden trees.

SEPTEMBER 29, 1870

Rêvé pour l'hiver

Á † † † Elle

L'hiver, nous irons dans un petit wagon rose
    Avec des coussins bleus.
Nous serons bien. Un nid de baisers fous repose
    Dans chaque coin moelleux.

Tu fermeras l'œil, pour ne point voir, par la glace,
    Grimacer les ombres des soirs,
Ces monstruosités hargneuses, populace
    De démons noirs et de loups noirs.

Puis tu te sentiras la joue égratignée...
Un petit baiser, comme une folle araignée,
    Te courra par le cou...

Et tu me diras: "Cherche!", en inclinant la tête,
—Et nous prendrons du temps à trouver cette bête
    —Qui voyage beaucoup...

En Wagon, le 7 octobre 70

A Dream of Winter

To † † † Her

In winter, we will leave in a small pink caboose
    strewn with soft blue cushions,
insanely comfortable, where nests of kisses roost
    in corners like children.

You'll shut your eyes, afraid of the changeling glass:
    the night shadows' faces
teeming, snarling, grotesque, an angry populace
    of black wolves and Satans.

Then, on your quaking cheek, you will feel a light scratch,
a wee kiss, like a spider that's lost its hat,
    will flit along your neck,

and you will shout, "Get it!," as you submit your head
—It will take seven weeks to snare that pesky brat
    —Who prefers a long trek...

    OCTOBER 7, 1870, ON A TRAIN

2: FIRST MARCHES

What you advised me not to do, I did: I left the maternal mansion and went to Paris! I was arrested as I got off the train for not having any money and owing thirteen francs on my ticket, and taken to the police station, and now I am in prison at Mazas waiting for trial!

—Rimbaud to Georges Izambard, September 5, 1870

Les chercheuses de poux

Quand le front de l'enfant, plein de rouges tourmentes,
Implore l'essaim blanc des rêves indistincts,
Il vient près de son lit deux grandes sœurs charmantes
Avec de frêles doigts aux ongles argentins.

Elles assoient l'enfant devant une croisée
Grande ouverte où l'air bleu baigne un fouillis de fleurs
Et dans ses lourds cheveux où tombe la rosée
Promènent leurs doigts fins, terribles et charmeurs.

Il écoute chanter leurs haleines craintives
Qui fleurent de longs miels végétaux et rosés
Et qu'interrompt parfois un sifflement, salives
Reprises sur la lèvre ou désirs de baisers.

Il entend leurs cils noirs battant sous les silences
Parfumés; et leurs doigts électriques et doux
Font crépiter parmi ses grises indolences
Sous leurs ongles royaux la mort des petits poux.

Voilà que monte en lui le vin de la Paresse,
Soupir d'harmonica qui pourrait délirer;
L'enfant se sent, selon la lenteur des caresses
Sourdre et mourir sans cesse un désir de pleurer.

The Seekers of Lice

When the child's forehead, cursed with furies, red blisters,
pines for a forgetful swarm of pathetic dreams,
there steps to his bed two rangy, highborn sisters
—silver nails extended from refined, slender limbs.

They fix the child in a chair before a window
showing on the blue air that bathes fecund meadows;
they drive, through hair matted with sweat and morning dew,
their charming, delicate fingers, cruel as new snow.

He hears their sibilance, their halting song, their breath
thick with honey odor, vegetable, roseate,
broken here and there by their spittle's sucked hisses,
their plays for kisses thwarted, stillborn, celibate.

He hears black eyelashes flutter in the perfumed
silence; their electric fingers craft paradise,
a half-drunk indolence, while through the humid room
crackle the royal nails crushing the little lice.

But then: the wine of Sloth rises in him; the sigh
of a harmonica bruises the azure sky.
The tympanic flows of their fingers catalyze,
surging, dying, surging in him—the need to cry.

1870-1872

Venus Anadyomène

Comme d'un cercueil vert en fer blanc, une tête
De femme à cheveux bruns fortement pommadés
D'une vieille baignoire émerge, lente et bête,
Avec des déficits assez mal ravaudés;

Puis le col gras et gris, les larges omoplates
Qui saillent; le dos court qui rentre et qui ressort;
Puis les rondeurs des reins semblent prendre l'essor;
La graisse sous la peau paraît en feuilles plates:

L'échine est un peu rouge, et le tout sent un goût
Horrible étrangement; on remarque surtout
Des singularités qu'il faut voir à la loupe...

Les reins poilent deux mots gravés: CLARA VENUS;
—Et tout ce corps remue et tend sa large croupe
Belle hideusement d'un ulcère à l'anus.

Venus Anadyomene

As if from a green tin coffin, the woman's head
rises, her hair piled with a thick, gooey pomade;
slowly, stupidly, it grows from an old bathtub
with bald patches only indifferently concealed.

Then, the neck—fat, gray—then, the giant shoulder blades
that jut out; then, curves and bulges of her small back;
then, the butt cheeks, spheroid, as if keen to escape
—the grease beneath the skin unfolds in rolling sheets.

The spine is a bit red; the whole show slightly reeks,
strangely awful. But one prizes, especially
things one only sees with a magnifying glass:

on the buttocks, two engraved words: CLARA VENUS,
and that whole body moves, extending its wide ass
—gorgeous! grotesque!—with an ulcer on the anus.

JULY 27, 1870

"Morts de Quatre-vingt-douze…"

"…Français de soixante-dix, bonapartistes, républicains, souvenez-vous
de vos pères en 92, etc.…" —Paul de Cassagnac *(Le pays)*

Morts de Quatre-vingt-douze et de Quatre-vingt-treize,
Qui, pâles du baiser fort de la liberté,
Calmes, sous vos sabots, brisiez le joug qui pèse
Sui l'âme et sur le front de toute humanité;

Homme extasiés et grands dans la tourmente,
Vous dont les cœurs sautaient d'amour sous les haillons,
O Soldats que la Mort a semés, noble Amante,
Pour les régénérer, dans tous les vieux sillons;

Vous dont le sang lavait toute grandeur salie,
Morts de Valmy, Morts de Fleurus, Morts d'Italie,
Ô million de Christs aux yeux sombres et doux;

Nous vous laissions dormir avec la République,
Nous, courbés sous les rois comme sous une trique:
—Messieurs de Cassagnac nous reparlent de vous!

Fait à Mazas, septembre 1870.

"Oh you dead of Ninety-two..."

"Frenchmen of 1870, Bonapartists, Republicans, remember
   your fathers in 92, etc...." —Paul de Cassagnac *(Le pays)*

Oh you dead of Ninety-two and Ninety-three who,
—pale from the brutal kiss you bore from Liberty—
crushed beneath your sabots the heavy, evil yoke
that bent the brow and soul of all humanity!

Noble, extraordinary Men! In that storm
your hearts sallied forth from under your stinking rags
—soldiers who Death, that noble Paramour, has sown
in dry furrows that, one day, you could rise again!

You who cleansed with your blood every defiled glory,
you, the dead of Valmy, of Fleurus, of Italy,
you, a million Christs with eyes mellow and earnest,

we have let you sleep, dormant with the Republic,
we, cowered under kings as under a nightstick
—Cassagnac's men exhume, once again, your corpses!

MADE IN THE MAZAS PRISON, SEPTEMBER 3, 1870

L'eclatante victoire de Sarrebrück

Remportée aux cris de vive l'empereur!
(Gravure belge brillamment coloriée, se vend à Charleroi, 35 centimes.)

Au milieu, l'Empereur dans une apothéose
Bleue et jaune, s'en va, raide, sur son dada
Flamboyant; très heureux,—car il voit tout en rose,
Féroce comme Zeus et doux comme un papa;

En bas, les bons Pioupious qui faisaient la sieste
Près des tambours dorés et des rouges canons,
Se lèvent gentiment. Pitou remet sa veste,
Et, tourné vers le Chef, s'étourdit de grands noms!

À droite, Dumanet, appuyé sur la crosse
De son chassepot, sent frémir sa nuque en brosse,
Et: "Vive l'Empereur!!"—Son voisin reste coi...

Un schako surgit, comme un soleil noir...—Au centre,
Boquillon rouge et bleu, très naïf, sur son ventre
Se dresse, et,—présentant ses derrières—: "De quoi?..."

The Dazzling Victory of Sarrebruck

Won to shouts of Long Live the Emperor!
(Belgian engraving, in dazzling colors on sale at Charleroi, 35 centimes)

Dead center: the Emperor, apotheosized
in yellow and blue, a-jingle on his *dada*;
flamboyant, cheerful, he sees all as rose-tinted
—he's ferocious as Zeus, and mild as a papa.

Below, his jolly Grunts, taking a siesta
near the gold-trimmed drums, the red cannons, the shakos;
—tipsily, they're astir. Pitou dons his jacket,
and, facing Chief, enthuses—fame-drunk on Heroes!

On the right, Dumanet, his rear against the butt
of his chassepot, feels the hair on his neck rise. He
blurts: "Long Live the Emperor!" —The others grumble...

A cap climbs, like a blackened sun... in the middle,
Bouquillon, red and blue, gut splayed, sweet idiot,
—raises his fat ass like a stool. —He asks: "On what?"

OCTOBER, 1870

Le dormeur du val

C'est un trou de verdure où chante une rivière
Accrochant follement aux herbes des haillons
D'argent; où le soleil, de la montagne fière,
Luit: c'est un petit val qui mousse de rayons.

Un soldat jeune, bouche ouverte, tête nue,
Et la nuque baignant dans le frais cresson bleu,
Dort; il est étendu dans l'herbe, sous la nue,
Pâle dans son lit vert où la lumière pleut.

Les pieds dans les glaïeuls, il dort. Souriant comme
Sourirait un enfant malade, il fait un somme:
Nature, berce-le chaudement: il a froid.

Les parfums ne font pas frissonner sa narine;
Il dort dans le soleil, la main sur sa poitrine
Tranquille. Il a deux trous rouges au côté droit.

Octobre 1870

The Sleeper in the Valley

It is a deep green vale where a small river sings,
leaving, impishly, its silver beads on the grass,
where the sun charges down from a proud mountain range
to flood the spot with rays of yellow-carat glass.

A young soldier, his lips parted, his head not capped,
the nape of his neck cool in the blue watercress,
sleeps; there, he extends on a gentle reedy slope;
light sinks from clouds to crown his pallid agelessness.

His feet recline in the gladiolas—he sleeps.
He smiles as a sick child would smile—he needs his rest.
Oh nature, gather him tightly! He's cold! He'll freeze!

Aromas of the vale don't wrench his nostrils wide.
He basks in the sun, an idle hand on his breast
—tranquil. Two red cavities yawn on his right side.

OCTOBER, 1870

Le mal

Tandis que les crachats rouges de la mitraille
Sifflent tout le jour par l'infini du ciel bleu;
Qu'écarlates ou verts, près du Roi qui les raille,
Croulent les bataillons en masse dans le feu;

Tandis qu'une folie épouvantable, broie
Et fait de cent milliers d'hommes un tas fumant;
—Pauvres morts! dans l'été, dans l'herbe, dans ta joie,
Nature! ô toi qui fis ces hommes saintement!...—

—Il est un Dieu, qui rit aux nappes damassées
Des autels, à l'encens, aux grands calices d'or;
Qui dans le bercement des hosannah s'endort,

Et se réveille, quand des mères, ramassées
Dans l'angoisse, et pleurant sous leur vieux bonnet noir,
Lui donnent un gros sou lié dans leur mouchoir!

Evil

While rifles emit their rose-red mists of grapeshot
whistling all day beneath the infinite blue sky,
dressed in scarlet and green, near a King who coolly mocks
their guts—entire troops disintegrate under fire.

While a terrible madness rages, and makes of boys,
a hundred thousand of them, a smoking trash heap
—You poor dead! in the grass, in summer, in your joy!
Nature! who venerates these boys—and deems them holy!

—There is a God. He laughs at the damask covers
on the altars, the incense, at the golden grails;
he takes a snooze while quaint lullabies Hosanna.

—Then he wakes, when the shy mothers come together
in anguish, slobbering under chintzy black veils.
—Each one shoves him pennies, tied up in a clean scarf!

1870

Rages de Césars

L'Homme pâle, le long des pelouses fleuries,
Chemine, en habit noir, et le cigare aux dents:
L'Homme pâle repense aux fleurs des Tuileries
—Et parfois son œil terne a des regards ardents...

Car l'Empereur est soûl de ses vingt ans d'orgie!
Il s'était dit: "Je vais souffler la Liberté
Bien délicatement, ainsi qu'une bougie!"
La Liberté revit! Il se sent éreinté!

Il est pris:—Oh! quel nom sur ses lèvres muettes
Tressaille? Quel regret implacable le mord?
On ne le saura pas. L'Empereur a l'œil mort.

Il repense peut-être au Compère en lunettes...
—Et regarde filer de son cigare en feu,
Comme aux soirs de Saint-Cloud, un fin nuage bleu.

Caesars' Rages

Along the flowering lawns, the Pale Emperor
walks. He wears a black coat, a cigar in his teeth.
The Pale Man reflects on the green, vanished gardens
of the Tuileries. At times, sobering, he sees…

—For the pale man is drunk! —His twenty-year orgy
has gone to his head! He'd once said: "Like a candle,
blowing—quite gently—I will huff out Liberty!"
But Liberty lives again! So he feels unwell.

He's imprisoned. —Oh, what is that name that hovers
on his lips? What implacable remorse slays him?
One will never know. The Emperor's eye is dim.

Perhaps, he recalls his spectacled Assistant.
—And he watches, rising from his burning cheroot,
thin blue whiffs, as in those old evenings at St. Cloud.

1870

Le buffet

C'est un large buffet sculpté; le chêne sombre,
Très vieux, a pris cet air si bon des vieilles gens;
Le buffet est ouvert, et verse dans son ombre
Comme un flot de vin vieux, des parfums engageants;

Tout plein, c'est un fouillis de vieilles vieilleries,
De linges odorants et jaunes, de chiffons
De femmes ou d'enfants, de dentelles flétries,
De fichus de grand-mère où sont peints des griffons;

—C'est là qu'on trouverait les médaillons, les mèches
De cheveux blancs ou blonds, les portraits, les fleurs sèches
Dont le parfum se mêle à des parfums de fruits.

—Ô buffet du vieux temps, tu sais bien des histoires,
Et tu voudrais conter tes contes, et tu bruis
Quand s'ouvrent lentement tes grandes portes noires.

octobre 70

The Sideboard

It is ample—a sideboard, sculpted from dark oak;
quite old, it has the delicate air of old folks;
the sideboard is open; wafting from its shadows
like cascades of old wine, sweet, suggestive odors.

Crammed to the full, chock-a-block with odd old knickknacks:
fragrant yellow linens; torn bits from the garments
of women or children; faded, tattered laces;
the scarves of grandmothers embroidered with griffins.

—There, you will discover: pearl medallions; cinched locks
of hair, white or blonde; palm-sized portraits; dried flowers,
their gray odors mingling with the odors of fruit.

—Oh, buffet of old times, you have many stories,
and, eager to relate your tales, you murmur, bark
when, like a rusted gate, your big black doors swing out!

OCTOBER, 1870

À la musique

Place de la gare, à Charleville

Sur la place taillée en mesquines pelouses,
Square où tout est correct, les arbres et les fleurs,
Tous les bourgeois poussifs qu'étranglent les chaleurs
Portent, les jeudis soir, leurs bêtises jalouses.

—L'orchestre militaire, au milieu du jardin,
Balance ses schakos dans la *Valse des fifres*:
—Autour, aux premiers rangs, parade le gandin;
Le notaire pend à ses breloques à chiffres:

Des rentiers à lorgnons soulignent tous les couacs:
Les gros bureaux bouffis traînent leurs grosses dames
Auprès desquelles vont, officieux cornacs,
Celles dont les volants ont des airs de réclames;

Sur les bancs verts, des clubs d'épiciers retraités
Qui tisonnent le sable avec leur canne à pomme,
Fort sérieusement discutent les traités,
Puis prisent en argent, et reprennent: "En somme!..."

Épatant sur son banc les rondeurs de ses reins,
Un bourgeois à boutons clairs, bedaine flamande,
Savoure son onnaing d'où le tabac par brins
Déborde—vous savez, c'est de la contrebande;—

Le long des gazons verts ricanent les voyous;
Et, rendus amoureux par le chant des trombones,
Très naïfs, et fumant des roses, les pioupious
Caressent les bébés pour enjôler les bonnes...

—Moi, je suis, débraillé comme un étudiant
Sous les marronniers verts les alertes fillettes:

Set to Music

The Station Square, Charleville

On this square carved into trivial plots of grass,
a square—manicured trees, flowers strictly to taste—
the wheezy bourgeois, stifled by incalescence,
drag each Thursday night their ridiculous envies.

—The military orchestra swings its shakos
to the Waltz of the Fifes inside the trimmed garden
—The Dandy struts his stuff, crowding out the front rows;
the notary dangles from his monogrammed fob.

Men of private means criticize all the false notes:
men from fat, swollen desks cart along their fat wives
near whom, like officious drivers of elephants,
women don flounces fluttering like endorsements.

On the green benches, cadres of retired grocers
tease lines in the sand with their knobby-headed canes;
they argue, gravely, the virtues of trade statutes,
take another pinch of tobacco—"Well, I say..."

Generously spreading his ass over a bench,
a bourgeois with shiny buttons, a Flemish paunch,
suckles an onnaing pipe, dangling from which are shreds
of hairy tobacco—he swears it's contraband...

Sniggering along the grass are the great loafers;
and, growing amorous to the songs of trombones,
very naive, chewing on roses, young soldiers
coddle pink tykes to get in good with shy nannies.

—And I? I'm dressed like an impoverished student
and trail, under the chestnut trees, the spry girls;

Elles le savent bien, et tournent en riant,
Vers moi, leurs yeux tout pleins de choses indiscrètes

Je ne dis pas un mot: je regarde toujours
La chair de leurs cous blancs brodés de mèches folles:
Je suis, sous le corsage et les frêles atours,
Le dos divin après la courbe des épaules

J'ai bientôt déniché la bottine, le bas...
—Je reconstruis les corps, brûlé de belles fièvres.
Elles me trouvent drôle et se parlent tout bas...
—Et je sens les baisers qui me viennent aux lèvres...

they are quite aware—they turn to me, laughing,
their eyes full of things indiscreet—not wholly rare!

I do not say a word. I continue to gaze
at the flash of their white necks framed by stray locks.
I trace, behind blouses—translucent fineries—
beneath their shoulders, the curves of their divine backs.

Soon, I have unearthed the ankle boot, the stocking...
burning with fine fevers, I reconstruct the whole
figure...—They find me amusing—they speak quite low—
and my fierce desires seize upon their straying mouths.

1870

La maline

Dans la salle à manger brune, que parfumait
Une odeur de vernis et de fruits, à mon aise
Je ramassais un plat de je ne sais quel met
Belge, et je m'épatais dans mon immense chaise.

En mangeant, j'écoutais l'horloge,—heureux et coi.
La cuisine s'ouvrit avec une bouffée
—Et la servante vint, je ne sais pas pourquoi,
Fichu moitié défait, malinement coiffée

Et, tout en promenant son petit doigt tremblant
Sur sa joue, un velours de pêche rose et blanc,
En faisant, de sa lèvre enfantine, une moue,

Elle arrangeait les plats, près de moi, pour m'aiser;
—Puis, comme ça,—bien sûr pour avoir un baiser—
Tout bas: "Sens donc, j'ai pris *une* froid sur la joue..."

Charleroi, octobre 70

The Sly Girl

In the brown dining room wafting with aromas
of turpentine and fruit, drowsily, at my ease,
I picked at my plate of Belgian, I think, hor d'oeuvres,
stretched out on my chair like a sultry Siamese.

I sat, I ate; the clock ticked its naive music.
But then—the kitchen door swung out with a sharp gust!
Friends, I don't know why, but the servant girl flew in
scarves disheveled, hair wild, enticingly careless.

She let a small, trembling finger span her soft cheek,
velvety, pink and white, savory as a peach;
she pouted, a hurt child, as if the fault were me.

She wiped the table, cleared it, apologetic;
but then, like that! she leaned toward me, like for a kiss,
hissing softly, "Feel here, I've *such* a frozen cheek."

OCTOBER, 1870, CHARLEROI

Au Cabaret-Vert

cinq heures du soir

Depuis huit jours, j'avais déchiré mes bottines
Aux cailloux des chemins. J'entrais à Charleroi.
—*Au Cabaret-Vert*: je demandai des tartines
De beurre et du jambon qui fût à moitié froid.

Bienheureux, j'allongeai les jambes sous la table
Verte: je contemplai les sujets très naïfs
De la tapisserie.—Et ce fut adorable,
Quand la fille aux tétons énormes, aux yeux vifs,

—Celle-là, ce n'est pas un baiser qui l'épeure!—
Rieuse, m'apporta des tartines de beurre,
Du jambon tiède, dans un plat colorié,

Du jambon rose et blanc parfumé d'une gousse
D'ail,—et m'emplit la chope immense, avec sa mousse
Que dorait un rayon de soleil arriéré.

Octobre 70

At The Cabaret-Vert

five in the afternoon

For eight lonely days I shredded my only boots
on pebbles on the roads. I entered Charleroi.
—*At the Cabaret-Vert*: I ordered simple toast,
a pat of butter, and ham that was barely warm.

I felt good. I stretched my legs under the long, green
table. I let my mind wander among the scenes
scrawled on the tapestries. This was solace. Serene.
Then, the girl with huge tits, eyes jumping like cocaine

—This one, I thought, is not quick to deny a kiss!—
giggling, carried to me on a cracked, colored dish
the lukewarm ham, butter, and bread not one day old,

ham pink and white, perfumed by sweetly acrid cloves
of garlic—and she filled my heavy mug with foam
which the late sun rays pierced, lit up with flames of gold.

OCTOBER, 1870

Ma bohème (Fantaisie)

Je m'en allais, les poings dans mes poches crevées;
Mon paletot aussi devenait idéal;
J'allais sous le ciel, Muse! et j'étais ton féal;
Oh! là! là! que d'amours splendides j'ai rêvées!

Mon unique culotte avait un large trou.
—Petit-Poucet rêveur j'égrenais dans ma course
Des rimes. Mon auberge était à la Grande-Ourse.
—Mes étoiles au ciel avaient un doux frou-frou

Et je les écoutais, assis au bord des routes,
Ces bons soirs de septembre où je sentais des gouttes
De rosée à mon front, comme un vin de vigueur;

Où, rimant au milieu des ombres fantastiques,
Comme des lyres, je tirais les élastiques
De mes souliers blessés, un pied près de mon cœur!

My Bohemian Life (Fantasy)

And so I went, my fists stuffed in my torn pockets,
my coat so shredded it was simply an Idea;
I trod beneath the sky, Muse! your willing servant
and oh! what brilliant loves my cinema unreeled!

I wore my only slacks—enhanced by a big hole.
A tiny, drunk Tom Thumb, I sowed as I rambled
my opalescent rhymes. My inn was Big Dipper;
beneath the curving sky, stars—my chorus—rustled.

I listened to them, crouched by country roads, alert,
those warm August nights, until dew mottled my face
like fortifying wine. And then, amidst milieus

of teeming blue shadows, I intoned my verses
strumming, as if a lyre, my withered shoelaces,
ribs of my wounded shoes! one foot beneath my heart.

1870

3: APPROACHING PARIS

I will be a worker: That's what holds me back when a wild fury drives me toward the battle in Paris, where so many workers are still dying while I am writing to you! Work, now? Never, never. I'm on strike.

—Rimbaud to Georges Izambard, May 17, 1871

Bal des pendus

Au gibet noir manchot aimable,
Dansent, dansent les paladins,
Les maigres paladins du diable,
Les squelettes de Saladins.

Messire Belzébuth tire par la cravate
Ses petits pantins noirs grimaçant sur le ciel,
Et, leur claquant au front un revers de savate,
Les fait danser danser aux sons d'un vieux Noël!

Et les pantins choqués enlacent leurs bras grêles:
Comme des orgues noirs, les poitrines à jour
Que serraient autrefois les gentes damoiselles,
Se heurtent longuement dans un hideux amour.

Hurrah! les gais danseurs, qui n'avez plus de panse!
On peut cabrioler les tréteaux sont si longs!
Hop! qu'on ne sache plus si c'est bataille ou danse!
Belzébuth enragé racle ses violons!

Ô durs talons, jamais on n'use sa sandale!
Presque tous ont quitté la chemise de peau:
Le reste est peu gênant et se voit sans scandale.
Sur les crânes, la neige applique un blanc chapeau:

Le corbeau fait panache à ces têtes fêlées,
Un morceau de chair tremble à leur maigre menton:
On dirait, tournoyant dans les sombres mêlées,
Des preux, raides, heurtant armures de carton.

Hurrah! La bise siffle au grand bal des squelettes!
Le gibet noir mugit comme un orgue de fer!
Les loups vont répondant des forêts violettes:
À l'horizon, le ciel est d'un rouge d'enfer…

Dance of the Hanged Men

Cheerful, black, one-armed gallows,
There dance, dance the heroes!
The devil's skinny paladins!
Like the skeletons of Saladins!

Monsieur Beelzebub dangles by their neckties
his little black puppets; they grimace at the sky.
He smacks their dark brows with his meaty hands' backsides
—sets them dancing, dancing, to the sounds of Noels!

And the puppets' arms, like hollow, black organ pipes,
entangle as they jostle—they group, get enmeshed
—a hideous love-making! Day shines through their breasts
on which, in rosier times, belle dames pressed their heads.

Ha! You, gay dancers! Divested of your flab!
These stages are so wide, you've room—experiment!
Hop! No need to ask if it's warfare or a dance!
Beelzebub—enraged, inspired—shreds his violin!

Oh, the hard heels! Who needs a shoe or a sandal!
Now, almost all remove their skin button-downs;
what's left is not too shabby—hardly a scandal!
On their skulls: the snow sets down a white sombrero.

A crow rests like a plume on these jigsaw-cracked heads;
a little piece of flesh dangles from their thin chins;
one could say, as they mingle in their dark contests,
that they're stiff knights clashing, wearing armor of tin.

Ha! The breeze whistles through this grand Skeleton Ball!
The black gibbet groans like an organ of iron!
On the horizon, the sky is the red of hell...
The wolves howl accompaniment from violet wolds.

Holà, secouez-moi ces capitans funèbres
Qui défilent, sournois, de leurs gros doigts cassés
Un chapelet d'amour sur leurs pâles vertèbres:
Ce n'est pas un moustier ici, les trépassés!

Oh! voilà qu'au milieu de la danse macabre
Bondit dans le ciel rouge un grand squelette fou
Emporté par l'élan, comme un cheval se cabre:
Et, se sentant encor la corde raide au cou,

Crispe ses petits doigts sur son fémur qui craque
Avec des cris pareils à des ricanements,
Et, comme un baladin rentre dans la baraque,
Rebondit dans le bal au chant des ossements.

    Au gibet noir manchot aimable,
    Dansent, dansent les paladins
    Les maigres paladins du diable,
    Les squelettes de Saladins.

Hey! Someone shake up those funereal sluggards
who, with their fat broken fingers, arrogantly
spread their rosaries across their white vertebrae!
—You! the Passed Away! This ain't no monastery!

Oh! There, in the middle of this dance macabre
a grand, maddened skeleton springs to the red sky,
a bit too zealous, like an Arabian horse,
and, still feeling the rope saddled around his spine,

clenches his small fingers around his thigh—it cracks
with cries similar to jeers... But like a clown who
retires to his room, but then suddenly leaps back
—he rejoins the dance to the singing of the bones!

    Cheerful, black, one-armed gallows,
    There dance, dance the heroes!
    The devil's skinny paladins!
    Like the skeletons of Saladins!

1870

Le forgeron

Palais des Tuileries, vers le 10 août 92

Le bras sur un marteau gigantesque, effrayant
D'ivresse et de grandeur, le front vaste, riant
Comme un clairon d'airain, avec toute sa bouche,
Et prenant ce gros-là dans son regard farouche,
Le Forgeron parlait à Louis Seize, un jour
Que le Peuple était là, se tordant tout autour,
Et sur les lambris d'or traînant sa veste sale.
Or le bon roi, debout sur son ventre, était pâle
Pâle comme un vaincu qu'on prend pour le gibet,
Et, soumis comme un chien, jamais ne regimbait
Car ce maraud de forge aux énormes épaules
Lui disait de vieux mots et des choses si drôles,
Que cela l'empoignait au front, comme cela!

"Or tu sais bien, Monsieur, nous chantions tra la la
Et nous piquions les bœufs vers les sillons des autres:
Le Chanoine au soleil filait des patenôtres
Sur des chapelets clairs grenés de pièces d'or
Le Seigneur, à cheval, passait, sonnant du cor
Et l'un avec la hart, l'autre avec la cravache
Nous fouaillaient.—Hébétés comme des yeux de vache,
Nos yeux ne pleuraient plus; nous allions, nous allions,
Et quand nous avions mis le pays en sillons,
Quand nous avions laissé dans cette terre noire
Un peu de notre chair... nous avions un pourboire
On nous faisait flamber nos taudis dans la nuit
Nos petits y faisaient un gâteau fort bien cuit.

..."Oh! je ne me plains pas. Je te dis mes bêtises,
C'est entre nous. J'admets que tu me contredises.
Or n'est-ce pas joyeux de voir, au mois de juin
Dans les granges entrer des voitures de foin

The Blacksmith

Palace of the Tuileries, about August 10, 1792

Laughing like a bronze trumpet, chilling in his girth
and broad brow, near a huge hammer on which he perched
an elbow—very drunk!—roaring from his great maw,
controlling the Fat Man with only his hard stare,
the Blacksmith spoke with Louis the Sixteenth that day
when the People were out, hurtling about their ways,
dragging their dirty coats across the gilt facades.
And now, the good King, like a flagpole wearing guts,
was pale, white as a victim nearing the gallows,
and, meek as a pup, he succumbed without a fuss
to that devil from the forge with his puffed-out chest
who flooded him with phrases so strange, so ancient,
that it grabbed him by the forelock, as if—voila!

"Now you know, dear Sir, how we used to sing tra la la,
as we led our oxen toward those furrows of theirs;
the Canon in the sun intoned his paternosters
fingering his rosary strung with beads of gold;
the Lord, high on his steed, blowing his horn, would scold
one peasant with a noose, the other with a whip,
—he lashed us! and though our cows' eyes glazed, we'd not weep
and we went on and on, on and on, until night,
until we had plowed the entire countryside;
and, by that time, we had left in the thick black dirt
a red mound of our flesh... For that, we got a perk:
our shacks were set aflame under shelter of dark,
our children—still sleeping!—baked into a fine tart.

"Oh, I'm not complaining! Just unloading my gush...
This is just between us! Contradict, if you wish!
But isn't it a joy to see, in pregnant June,
to see the wagons entering, impressive, huge,

Énormes? De sentir l'odeur de ce qui pousse,
Des vergers quand il pleut un peu, de l'herbe rousse?
De voir des blés, des blés, des épis pleins de grain,
De penser que cela prépare bien du pain?...
Oh! plus fort, on irait, au fourneau qui s'allume,
Chanter joyeusement en martelant l'enclume,
Si l'on était certain de pouvoir prendre un peu,
Étant homme, à fin! de ce que donne Dieu!
—Mais voilà, c'est toujours la même vieille histoire!...

"Mais je sais, maintenant! Moi, je ne peux plus croire,
Quand j'ai deux bonnes mains, mon front et mon marteau,
Qu'un homme vienne là, dague sur le manteau,
Et me dise: Mon gars, ensemence ma terre;
Que l'on arrive encor, quand ce serait la guerre,
Me prendre mon garçon comme cela, chez moi!
—Moi, je serais un homme, et toi, tu serais roi,
Tu me dirais: Je veux!...—Tu vois bien, c'est stupide.
Tu crois que j'aime voir ta baraque splendide,
Tes officiers dorés, tes mille chenapans,
Tes palsembleu bâtards tournant comme des paons:
Ils ont rempli ton nid de l'odeur de nos filles
Et de petits billets pour nous mettre aux Bastilles,
Et nous dirons: C'est bien: les pauvres à genoux!
Nous dorerons ton Louvre en donnant nos gros sous!
Et tu te soûleras, tu feras belle fête.
—Et ces Messieurs riront, les reins sur notre tête!

"Non. Ces saletés-là datent de nos papas!
Oh! Le Peuple n'est plus une putain. Trois pas
Et tous, nous avons mis ta Bastille en poussière
Cette bête suait du sang à chaque pierre
Et c'était dégoûtant, la Bastille debout
Avec ses murs lépreux qui nous racontaient tout
Et, toujours, nous tenaient enfermés dans leur ombre!
—Citoyen! citoyen! c'était le passé sombre
Qui croulait, qui râlait, quand nous prîmes la tour!

the bustling barns? to smell the odors as they waft
from orchards when it's drizzling, hay bales in the loft?
To see the wheat—and more wheat!—piled ears of corn,
and think about the bread the year's harvest will form?
And that, so much stronger, we'll trudge to the bright forge
and sing joyously as the hammer bleeds its sparks,
certain that, one day, we could make a pittance,
for, in the end, we are men! and of God's largesse!
—Eh, but, whatever... it's the same old tired story...

"Yet, now—I know! It's impossible to believe
when I have my strong hands, my mind, wielding my tools,
that a man can approach me, a knife in his folds,
and say to me: 'Boy, time now you plow my furrows!'
Or that someone can come, when war is afoot,
and rip my son away from under my ceiling!
Now, if I were a man, say, and you were the King,
you would say to me: That's great!... But no, it's stupid!
You think I like seeing your tall barns, so splendid,
your officers in gold, your thousand sycophants,
your strutting peacock what-the-fucks, thoughtless as ants?
They've filled your beds with the odors of our daughters,
condemned us to Bastilles with counterfeit letters,
and we will say: 'That's fine, all you poor, bend your knee!'
And we will guild your Louvres with our fat pennies,
and we will get drunk, indulge in our lowly fêtes
—and these Gentlemen will laugh, sitting on our heads!

"No, all that garbage dates from our fathers' era
—the People are no longer whores! Three steps forward,
and all of us have brought your Bastille to the ground.
That beast sweated blood from the last of its old stones,
and it was disgusting, the Bastille when erect,
with its leprous walls narrating like an old novel,
still keeping us enclosed within its dark hallways...
—Citizen! Citizen! it's our shared histories
that crumbled, croaking their last, when we stormed the walls,

Nous avions quelque chose au cœur comme l'amour.
Nous avions embrassé nos fils sur nos poitrines.
Et, comme des chevaux, en soufflant des narines
Nous allions, fiers et forts, et ça nous battait là...
Nous marchions au soleil, front haut,—comme cela—,
Dans Paris! On venait devant nos vestes sales.
Enfin! Nous nous sentions Hommes! Nous étions pâles,
Sire, nous étions soûls de terribles espoirs:
Et quand nous fûmes là, devant les donjons noirs,
Agitant nos clairons et nos feuilles de chêne,
Les piques à la main; nous n'eûmes pas de haine,
—Nous nous sentions si forts, nous voulions être doux!
. . . .

. . . .

"Et depuis ce jour-là, nous sommes comme fous!
Le tas des ouvriers a monté dans la rue,
Et ces maudits s'en vont, foule toujours accrue
De sombres revenants, aux portes des richards.
Moi, je cours avec eux assommer les mouchards:
Et je vais dans Paris, noir, marteau sur l'épaule,
Farouche, à chaque coin balayant quelque drôle,
Et, si tu me riais au nez, je te tuerais!
—Puis, tu peux y compter, tu te feras des frais
Avec tes hommes noirs, qui prennent nos requêtes
Pour se les renvoyer comme sur des raquettes
Et, tout bas, les malins! se disent: "Qu'ils sont sots!"
Pour mitonner des lois, coller de petits pots
Pleins de jolis décrets roses et de droguailles,
S'amuser à couper proprement quelques tailles.
Puis se boucher le nez quand nous marchons près d'eux,
—Nos doux représentants qui nous trouvent crasseux!—
Pour ne rien redouter, rien, que les baïonnettes...,
C'est très bien. Foin de leur tabatière à sornettes!
Nous en avons assez, là, de ces cerveaux plats
Et de ces ventres-dieux. Ah! ce sont là les plats
Que tu nous sers, bourgeois, quand nous sommes féroces,

we had something like love animating our souls,
and had embraced our sons and held them to our breasts,
and, like raging stallions, snorting steam through our snouts,
we went on, fiery and proud, hearts wildly pounding...
we marched in the sun, chins held high—to you down there
in Paris! They came to meet us in our soiled coats,
at last! We felt like Men! Drunk on terrible hopes,
we were pale, my dear Sir, light-headed, needing sleep:
and when we stood there, before the shadowy keeps,
waving our brass bugles and our branches of oak,
gripping our pikes!—strangely... nothing was left to loathe!
—We felt ourselves so strong, we wanted to be kind!

. . . .

. . . .

"And since that awareness, we've gone on like a mad wind,
the count of workers surging on the boulevards;
those haunted souls spun off in swelling, tireless crowds
of cursed phantoms, knocking at the doors of the rich.
And me? I run along, to finger the snitches:
so I run through Paris, hammer in arm, face black,
wild, in every street, muscling out cowardly scabs.
Had you laughed in my face? I would simply kill you.
—There's one thing you can be sure of: it will cost you
with your men in black who receive our petitions
and then bat them around like in a game of badminton,
and in sly low voices whisper, 'Oh, they're such fools!'
and enact fake laws, place the bills on weathered poles
full of pretty pink edicts and sweet placebos
and amuse themselves by cutting yet more zeros,
then pinching their nostrils as we walked right by them,
—Our kind Representatives, who think we're just scum!—
to assuage their fears of the thrusting bayonet...
That's fine. Let's get rid of the vapid press conference,
we've had enough of these lying, vacant pinheads,
these gods of the full stomach. These are the dishes
you bourgeois serve us when we, high in our madness,

Quand nous brisons déjà les sceptres et les crosses!..."

. . . .

Il le prend par le bras, arrache le velours
Des rideaux, et lui montre en bas les larges cours
Où fourmille, où fourmille, où se lève la foule,
La foule épouvantable avec des bruits de houle,
Hurlant comme une chienne, hurlant comme une mer,
Avec ses bâtons forts et ses piques de fer
Ses tambours, ses grands cris de halles et de bouges,
Tas sombre de haillons saignant de bonnets rouges:
L'Homme, par la fenêtre ouverte, montre tout
Au roi pâle et suant qui chancelle debout,
Malade à regarder cela!
                              "C'est la Crapule,
Sire. Ça bave aux murs, ça monte, ça pullule:
—Puisqu'ils ne mangent pas, Sire, ce sont des gueux!
Je suis un forgeron: ma femme est avec eux,
Folle! Elle croit trouver du pain aux Tuileries!
—On ne veut pas de nous dans les boulangeries.
J'ai trois petits. Je suis crapule.—Je connais
Des vieilles qui s'en vont pleurant sous leurs bonnets
Parce qu'on leur a pris leur garçon ou leur fille:
C'est la crapule.—Un homme était à la Bastille,
Un autre était forçat: et tous deux, citoyens
Honnêtes. Libérés, ils sont comme des chiens:
On les insulte! Alors, ils ont là quelque chose
Qui leur l'ait mal, allez! C'est terrible, et c'est cause
Que se sentant brisés, que, se sentant damnés,
Ils sont là, maintenant, hurlant sous votre nez!
Crapule.—Là-dedans sont des filles, infâmes,
Parce que,—vous saviez que c'est faible, les femmes,—
Messeigneurs de la cour,—que ça veut toujours bien,—
Vous [leur] avez craché sur l'âme, comme rien!
Vos belles, aujourd'hui, sont là. C'est la crapule.

. . . .

are snapping in half gold scepters and croziers...!"

. . . .

He takes him by the arm, throws open the velvet
drapes, aims his gaze down to the swelling courtyards
where the masses seethe and seethe, about to erupt
with the sound of hurricanes slowly building up,
howling like a flayed bitch, howling like an ocean,
their iron pikes and thick batons clashing, the din
from their drums, screaming from their markets and their shacks,
a dross of tattered rags blood-speckled with red caps:
the Blacksmith, through the open window, shows all this
to the pale sweating King now wobbly in his knees
sick at seeing that!
                    "Sir, that is the living Scum,
it slobbers on the walls, it rises, it squirms,
—since they are all famished, they're reduced to beggars.
I am a blacksmith; my wife, she's part of that swarm...
—crazy! She thinks she'll find bread in the Tuileries!
But we can't get within yards of their bakeries.
I have three little ones. I am scum. I have heard
of old women who weep under their dark bonnets
because their son or daughter was taken. So what!
—we are the scum. One man was put in the prison,
the other, a low-rent convict—but know, each bloke
is an honest citizen. Now, freed, they are dogs
that one despises! So, they have that thing that gnaws
at their simple hearts. It's awful! It is the cause
why they—feeling shattered, hounded like the accursed—
why they are here now—howling under your thin nose.
Scum. There are girls down there, many quite infamous
because they... well, you noble of the court, you know
how girls will tally their receipts, then come to you.
—You spat on their souls, as if they were worth nothing!
Down there, you see your belles out today. They are scum.

. . . .

"Oh! tous les Malheureux, tous ceux dont le dos brûle
Sous le soleil féroce, et qui vont, et qui vont,
Qui dans ce travail-là sentent crever leur front
Chapeau bas, mes bourgeois! Oh! ceux-là, sont les Hommes!
Nous sommes Ouvriers, Sire! Ouvriers! Nous sommes
Pour les grands temps nouveaux où l'on voudra savoir,
Où l'Homme forgera du matin jusqu'au soir
Chasseur des grands effets, chasseur des grandes causes,
Où, lentement vainqueur, il domptera les choses
Et montera sur Tout, comme sur un cheval!
Oh! splendides lueurs des forges! Plus de mal,
Plus!—Ce qu'on ne sait pas, c'est peut-être terrible:
Nous saurons!—Nos marteaux en main, passons au crible
Tout ce que nous savons: puis, Frères, en avant!
Nous faisons quelquefois ce grand rêve émouvant
De vivre simplement, ardemment, sans rien dire
De mauvais, travaillant sous l'auguste sourire
D'une femme qu'on aime avec un noble amour:
Et l'on travaillerait fièrement tout le jour,
Écoutant le devoir comme un clairon qui sonne:
Et l'on se sentirait très heureux: et personne,
Oh! personne, surtout, ne vous ferait ployer!
On aurait un fusil au-dessus du foyer...
. . . .

"Oh! mais l'air est tout plein d'une odeur de bataille!
Que te disais-je donc? Je suis de la canaille!
Il reste des mouchards et des accapareurs.
Nous sommes libres, nous! nous avons des terreurs
Où nous nous sentons grands, oh! si grands! Tout à l'heure
Je parlais de devoir calme, d'une demeure...
Regarde donc le ciel!—C'est trop petit pour nous,
Nous crèverions de chaud, nous serions à genoux!
Regarde donc le ciel!—Je rentre dans la foule,
Dans la grande canaille effroyable, qui roule,
Sire, tes vieux canons sur les sales pavés:
—Oh! quand nous serons morts, nous les aurons lavés

"Oh! all you wretches! whose backs burn under a sun
searing and ferocious, and go on, and go on,
who, in your labors, feel your heads about to blow,
take off your hats, oh, my bourgeois! Look! These are Men!
We are the workers, Sir. We are workers! We intend
future times when historians will want to know
who these Men were who forged—at midnight, in the noon—
hunters of new effects, hunters of new causes,
when, slowly victorious, he will tame all thoughts
and mount Everything, as one mounts a prize horse!
Oh, the splendid red glow of the forges! No more
evil—no more!—and though the unknown is frightening,
yet, we will know it! Hammers in hands, we will think
through all this new knowledge—and so, Brothers, forward!
On occasion, we will rest in that dream garden,
of a simple life lived with passion, with no word
of evil, working under the solemn regard
of a woman who we love with a noble love.
And we would work, proudly, the long day through, no slave,
but listening—like to a trumpet—to Duty:
and we will feel happy. Oh, there's really no way
that anyone—anyone at all—could make us
bend down. We'll have a loaded gun above our hearths...
. . . .

"Oh, the air is thick with the smells of battle!
—I'm sorry, what was I saying? I am from the swell,
and there are some left to pluck—informers and sharks.
But we are free. Yes, we do feel slightly berserk
because we feel great! So great! Just minutes ago
I spoke of peaceful Duty, of a quiet home...
Oh look at the sky! It is far too small for us,
we would die of heat, or collapse to our haunches!
Oh look at the sky! I'm returning to the crowd,
of the huge terrible mob, sir, that drags around
your old cannon over the dirty cobblestones—
Oh, when we are dead, we will mop them, bright and clean!

—Et si, devant nos cris, devant notre vengeance,
Les pattes des vieux rois mordorés, sur la France
Poussent leurs régiments en habits de gala,
Eh bien, n'est-ce pas, vous tous? Merde à ces chiens-là!"
. . . .

—Il reprit son marteau sur l'épaule.
                                        La foule
Près de cet homme-là se sentait l'âme soûle,
Et, dans la grande cour dans les appartements,
Où Paris haletait avec des hurlements,
Un frisson secoua l'immense populace
Alors, de sa main large et superbe de crasse
Bien que le roi ventru suât, le Forgeron,
Terrible, lui jeta le bonnet rouge au front!

—And if, against our complaints, against our vengeance,
the claws of old bronzed kings instigate throughout France
their regiments in full regalia to take march
—Well, isn't that just what you do. Fuck the Monarch!"
. . . .

He put the hammer back on his shoulder.
                                             The crowd
near him swooned, drunken, dizzily bolder. Somehow,
in that grand courtyard, in the tiny apartments,
as Paris panted with its hurled admonishments,
a shudder—sharp, immense—rang through the populace.
Then, with his broad hands impressively caked with ash,
the Blacksmith grabbed the potbellied King, and—madness!—
—just like that! he dropped on the King's head his scarlet!

1870

Les douaniers

Ceux qui disent: Cré Nom, ceux qui disent macache,
Soldats, marins, débris d'Empire, retraités
Sont nuls, très nuls, devant les Soldats des Traités
Oui tailladent l'azur frontière à grands coups d'hache

Pipe aux dents, lame en main, profonds, pas embêtés
Quand l'ombre bave aux bois comme un mufle de vache
Ils s'en vont, amenant leurs dogues à l'attache,
Exercer nuitamment leurs terribles gaîtés!

Ils signalent aux lois modernes les faunesses
Ils empoignent les Fausts et les Diavolos
«Pas de ça, les anciens! Déposez les ballots!"

Quand sa sérénité s'approche des jeunesses,
Le Douanier se tient aux appas contrôlés!
Enfer aux Délinquants que sa paume a frôlés!

The Customs Men

Those who say: *In God's name.* Those who say: *Pure bollocks!*
Soldiers, marines, the dregs of empire, retirees
are nothing—diddly—to Protectors of Treaties
who slash the frontier azure with the swing of an ax!

When darkness slobbers down the trees like cows' spittle,
pipes in teeth, blades in hands, serious, impassive,
they sally forth, dragging on leashes huge mastiffs,
to practice every night their harrowing revels!

They report the Lady Faun to our modern courts.
They grab all the Fausts and Devils—and pummel them!
—"Stop what you're doing, you antiques! Drop your bundles!"

But it's when Your Highness descends upon young boys...
the Customs Man, sensing tariffable items...
—Hell for the Delinquents whom his palms will fondle!

1870-1872

Chant de guerre parisien

Le Printemps est évident, car
Du cœur des Propriétés vertes,
Le vol de Thiers et de Picard
Tient ses splendeurs grandes ouvertes!

Ô Mai! quels délirants culs-nus!
Sèvres, Meudon, Bagneux, Asnières
Écoutez donc les bienvenus
Semer les choses printanières!

Ils ont schako, sabre et tam-tam,
Non la vieille boîte à bougies
Et des yoles qui n'ont jam, jam...
Fendent le lac aux eaux rougies!

Plus que jamais nous bambochons
Quand viennent sur nos tanières
Crouler les jaunes cabochons
Dans des aubes particulières!

Thiers et Picard sont des Éros,
Des enleveurs d'héliotropes,
Au pétrole ils font des Corots
Voici hannetonner leurs tropes...

Ils sont familiers du Grand Truc!...
Et couché dans les glaïeuls, Favre
Fait son cillement aqueduc,
Et ses reniflements à poivre!

La Grand ville a le pavé chaud,
Malgré vos douches de pétrole,
Et, décidément, il nous faut
Vous secouer dans votre rôle...

Parisian War Song

It is evident Spring's here, for
the verdant Estates hold wide
agape their amazing splendors
with the flight of Thiers and Picard!

Oh May! What delirious asses!
Sèvres, Meudon, Bagneux, Asnières,
listen now to the trespasses
that strew their spring-like cheers!

They have shakos, sabers, tom-toms,
not the old candle boxes,
and skiffs that have not ev-... ev-... um?
split lakes of bloodstained waters!

More than ever, we drink and dance
when, clambering our ant-warrens,
the yellow crania collapse
in these extraordinary dawns!

Thiers and Picard are twin Erotes
and thieves of heliotropes.
They paint Corots with petrol;
here, beetling about, are their tropes.

They're friends with the Grand Whozit!
—Favre, lounging in gladiolas,
blinking, weeps an aqueduct,
—his sniffles produce a pepper!

The Big City's cobbles are hot
in spite of your rains of oil;
and, decidedly, it's time that we
shuffle you up in your roles...

Et les Ruraux qui se prélassent
Dans de longs accroupissements,
Entendront des rameaux qui cassent
Parmi les rouges froissements!

And the Rustics who find solace
in long, luxurious squattings,
will hear, among red rustlings,
boughs in the forests snapping.

1871

L'orgie parisienne ou Paris se repeuple

Ô lâches, la voilà! dégorgez dans les gares!
Le soleil expia de ses poumons ardents
Les boulevards qu'un soir comblèrent les Barbares.
Voilà la Cité belle assise à l'occident!

Allez! on préviendra les reflux d'incendie,
Voilà les quais! voilà les boulevards! voilà,
Sur les maisons, l'azur léger qui s'irradie,
Et qu'un soir la rougeur des bombes étoila.

Cachez les palais morts dans des niches de planches!
L'ancien jour effaré rafraîchit vos regards.
Voici le troupeau roux des tordeuses de hanches,
Soyez fous, vous serez drôles, étant hagards!

Tas de chiennes en rut mangeant des cataplasmes,
Le cri des maisons d'or vous réclame. Volez!
Mangez! voici la nuit de joie aux profonds spasmes
Qui descend dans la rue, ô buveurs désolés,

Buvez. Quand la lumière arrive intense et folle
Fouillant à vos côtés les luxes ruisselants,
Vous n'allez pas baver, sans geste, sans parole,
Dans vos verres, les yeux perdus aux lointains blancs,

Avalez, pour la Reine aux fesses cascadantes!
Écoutez l'action des stupides hoquets
Déchirants. Écoutez, sauter aux nuits ardentes
Les idiots râleux, vieillards, pantins, laquais!

Ô cœurs de saleté, Bouches épouvantables
Fonctionnez plus fort, bouches de puanteurs!
Un vin pour ces torpeurs ignobles, sur ces tables...
Vos ventres sont fondus de hontes, ô Vainqueurs!

Parisian Orgy, or Paris is Repopulated

Oh cowards, pour into the stations! —Here she is!
The sun, its lungs afire, breathed its expiation
on the streets that, one night, roared with Barbarians.
—Oh pretty City! Jewel of the Occident!

Come! We will prevent the rekindling of the fire;
here are the quays! here, the boulevards! here, the homes
irradiated by the blue of the pale sky,
which, one night, were celestial with reddened bombs!

Bury the dusty, dark palaces beneath boards
—this frantic, ancient day refreshes your vision.
What's this? Some ginger-haired troop jiggles their rear ends!
Knock yourself out, folks, go nuts—no inhibitions!

Mangy bitches in heat gorging on poultices,
—the golden estates call you! Break in! Go kleptic!
Eat! Here, the joyous night, with uncontrollable spasms,
spans the whole avenue! Oh, born alcoholics

drink! When the light arrives, intense and lunatic,
streaming like luxury piercing your hook-bent spines,
will you not drool—eyes lost in the milky distance—
into your scraping glasses, mute, paralyzed?

Raise one for the Queen, her voluminous white ass!
Revel in the waves of sound, belch that rips through flesh,
on amorous nights, the huffing of idiots,
morons pirouetting, puppets, dupes, and old men!

Oh vile, salacious hearts! Oh terrifying mouths!
Work a little harder, oh foul-odored mouths!
More wine here for these base torpors, fill the tables!
Your entrails curl with bile in shame—oh Conquerers!

Ouvrez votre narine aux superbes nausées,
Trempez de poisons forts les cordes de vos cous,
Sur vos nuques d'enfants baissant ses mains croisées
Le Poète vous dit: ô lâches, soyez fous!

Parce que vous fouillez le ventre de la Femme
Vous craignez d'elle encore une convulsion
Qui crie, asphyxiant votre nichée infâme
Sur sa poitrine, en une horrible pression.

Syphilitiques, fous, rois, pantins, ventriloques,
Qu'est-ce que ça peut faire à la putain Paris,
Vos âmes et vos corps, vos poisons et vos loques?
Elle se secouera de vous, hargneux pourris!

Et quand vous serez bas, geignant sur vos entrailles
Les flancs morts, réclamant votre argent, éperdus,
La rouge courtisane aux seins gros de batailles,
Loin de votre stupeur tordra ses poings ardus!

Quand tes pieds ont dansé si fort dans les colères,
Paris! quand tu reçus tant de coups de couteau,
Quand tu gis, retenant dans tes prunelles claires,
Un peu de la bonté du fauve renouveau,

Ô cité douloureuse, ô cité quasi-morte,
La tête et les deux seins jetés vers l'Avenir
Ouvrant sur ta pâleur ses milliards de portes,
Cité que le Passé sombre pourrait bénir:

Corps remagnétisé pour les énormes peines,
Tu rebois donc la vie effroyable! tu sens
Sourdre le flux des vers livides en tes veines,
Et sur ton clair amour rôder les doigts glaçants!

Et ce n'est pas mauvais. Tes vers, tes vers livides
Ne gêneront pas plus ton souffle de Progrès

Open your nostrils wide, savor the fine vomit!
Soak the cords in your necks with rare, high class toxins!
The Poet implores you, as he rests his crossed hands
on your pubescent necks: Oh cowards! Go insane!

Because you still cry out for the womb of Woman,
nothing frightens more than an encore contraction
asphyxiating you, ripping you shrieking from
your infamous perch on her breast—dire compression!

Kings, fools, pawns, syphilitics, ventriloquists,
why should Paris the whore give two gold-plated shites
about your souls, bodies, poisons, rags and beds?
She'll just tell you to go fuck off, you surly pests.

And when, moaning, you grovel, clenching your doleful guts,
asking for your cash, your sides numb, vexed, out of it,
that scarlet courtesan with war-befattened bust
will keep a cool distance, shaking her iron fist.

In that time, when your feet danced in righteous fury,
—Paris! you were knifed, knifed again, wounds twice bleeding,
with your back stretched on the rack, with clear eyes you'd glean
a siren benevolence in young, russet Spring.

Oh suffering city, city half in the grave!
Your head and breasts leaning toward a regal Future
that accepts your stately limp through its million gates,
city who only the Past blesses with a pure word—

Corpse remagnetized for an intense, cleansing pain,
you redrink from wretched life! And then your senses
feel a tsunami of worms coursing through your veins,
—icy fingers that stalk the wrists of your one love.

This is not a bad thing! Those worms, pale and livid,
will not stifle the breath of Progress, will blind no eye

Que les Stryx n'éteignaient l'œil des Cariatides
Où des pleurs d'or astral tombaient des bleus degrés.

Quoique ce soit affreux de te revoir couverte
Ainsi; quoiqu'on n'ait fait jamais d'une cité
Ulcère plus puant à la Nature verte,
Le Poète te dit: "Splendide est ta Beauté!"

L'orage a sacrée ta suprême poésie;
L'immense remuement des forces te secourt;
Ton œuvre bout, la mort gronde, Cité choisie!
Amasse les strideurs au cœur du clairon lourd.

Le Poète prendra le sanglot des Infâmes,
La haine des Forçats, la clameur des maudits:
Et ses rayons d'amour flagelleront les Femmes.
Ses strophes bondiront: voilà! voilà! bandits!

—Société, tout est rétabli: les orgies
Pleurent leur ancien râle aux anciens lupanars:
Et les gaz en délire aux murailles rougies
Flambent sinistrement vers les azurs blafards!

Mai 1871.

any more than the Styx gouged the Caryatids
whose golden astral tears fell from the azure sky.

Though it's crippling to see you so foul, overrun
again; though there is no precedent, a city
so ulcerous, pus-drenched, in green nature, not one!
—The Poet cries to you: "Splendid is your Beauty!"

The floods have granted you the title: Pure Poetry.
A deep vitality carries you on its crest.
Your works seethe, death recoils, oh arrogant City!
Take into your strong heart fusillades of trumpets.

The Poet will take the howls of the Infamous,
the bile of the Convicts, the clangor of the Cursed.
His radiating Love will torment proud Woman.
His stanzas will bound forth—Look here, look here, you crooks!

—Society, all is restored! Orgies are crying
their ancient blubbering in ancient whorehouses.
On red-hued walls, gas lamps flicker their one frenzy,
sinisterly reaching toward the blue firmament.

MAY, 1871

4: HERESIES

"I am absolutely thwarted. Not a book, not a bar within reach, not an incident in the street. How horrible this French countryside is! My fate depends on this book [*A Season in Hell*], for which I still have to invent a half-dozen atrocious stories. How can I invent atrocities here?"

—Rimbaud to Ernest Delahaye, May, 1873

Le châtiment de Tartufe

Tisonnant, tisonnant son cœur amoureux sous
Sa chaste robe noire, heureux, la main gantée,
Un jour qu'il s'en allait, effroyablement doux,
Jaune, bavant la foi de sa bouche édentée,

Un jour qu'il s'en allait, "Oremus,"—un Méchant
Le prit rudement par son oreille benoîte
Et lui jeta des mots affreux, en arrachant
Sa chaste robe noire autour de sa peau moite!

Châtiment!... Ses habits étaient déboutonnés,
Et le long chapelet des péchés pardonnés
S'égrenant dans son cœur, Saint Tartufe était pâle!...

Donc, il se confessait, priait, avec un râle!
L'homme se contenta d'emporter ses rabats...
—Peuh! Tartufe était nu du haut jusques en bas!

Tartuffe's Punishment

His lustful heart raked, raked again, through coals beneath
his chaste black robe, joyful, donning a single glove,
as he ambled one day, amiable, oh so sweet,
yellow—drooling piety from his toothless jowls...

—As he ambled one day—"Le' us pray!"—an awful
fellow cuffed him roughly, dragging him by an ear,
and hurled a caustic deluge at him, assaulting
his chaste black robe—and exposing his sweating rear!

Now this was punishment! His clothes were unbuttoned,
and a long rosary—exonerated sins—
echoed within his heart. Saint Tartuffe turned ashen.

So, he confessed—he prayed—he shook a death rattle!
Buck naked, wow!—Tartuffe froze like a mannequin.
And the man, self-possessed, walked off with the clothes pile.

1870

Accroupissements

Bien tard, quand il se sent l'estomac écœuré,
Le frère Milotus, un œil à la lucarne
D'où le soleil, clair comme un chaudron récuré,
Lui darde une migraine et fait son regard darne,
Déplace dans les draps son ventre de curé

Il se démène sous sa couverture grise
Et descend, ses genoux à son ventre tremblant,
Effaré comme un vieux qui mangerait sa prise,
Car il lui faut, le poing à l'anse d'un pot blanc,
À ses reins largement retrousser sa chemise!

Or, il s'est accroupi, frileux, les doigts de pied
Repliés, grelottant au clair soleil qui plaque
Des jaunes de brioche aux vitres de papier;
Et le nez du bonhomme où s'allume la laque
Renifle aux rayons, tel qu'un charnel polypier.
. . . .

Le bonhomme mijote au feu, bras tordus, lippe
Au ventre: il sent glisser ses cuisses dans le feu,
Et ses chausses roussir, et s'éteindre sa pipe;
Quelque chose comme un oiseau remue un peu
À son ventre serein comme un monceau de tripe!

Autour, dort un fouillis de meubles abrutis
Dans des haillons de crasse et sur de sales ventres;
Des escabeaux, crapauds étranges, sont blottis
Aux coins noirs: des buffets ont des gueules de chantres
Qu'entrouvre un sommeil plein d'horribles appétits.

L'écœurante chaleur gorge la chambre étroite;
Le cerveau du bonhomme est bourré de chiffons:

Squattings

Late in the day, when he feels his stomach sicken,
Brother Milotus—one eye fixed to the skylight
through which the sun, clean like a scoured frying pan,
shoots a migraine at him, desolating his sight—
wriggles his curate's gut in his bed's deep cotton.

Under his gray blanket, antsy, he squirms about
—then gets up, his belly trembling against his knees,
frightened like a codger who had swallowed his quid,
because he has to raise his layer of PJs
to his hips as he grasps the ivory chamberpot!

When he has squatted, he is cold, and keeps his toes
pertly upturned; he shivers in the hard sunlight
that daubs the paper windowpanes with cake yellow.
This old fellow's nose, a roseate lacquer on fire,
snuffles at the sun's rays like a fleshy polyp.

. . . .

The old man simmers on the fire, arms crossed, flab lips
on his gut, and thinks: that his thighs might slip into
the fire—that his pants might scorch—that he needs to light
his pipe! Then, something like a bird begins to stir
in his dormant belly—like a mountain of tripe!

Around him are scads of moronic furniture
covered in greasy rags, over dirty bellies.
One-leggéd stools, strange toads, cower in the corners
and ancient sideboards yawn with the mouths of cantors
emboldened by a sleep of terrible desires.

The sickening heat fills the narrow, dusty place;
the old man's brain is stuffed with moldy, colored rags;

Il écoute les poils pousser dans sa peau moite,
Et parfois, en hoquets fort gravement bouffons
S'échappe, secouant son escabeau qui boite...
. . . .

Et le soir, aux rayons de lune, qui lui font
Aux contours du cul des bavures de lumière,
Une ombre avec détails s'accroupit, sur un fond
De neige rose ainsi qu'une rose trémière...
Fantasque, un nez poursuit Vénus au ciel profond.

he hears his hair crowding on moist epidermis.
At times, with bursts of seriously clownish hiccups,
he explodes—shaking his rickety wood footrest!

. . . .

In the night, the moon's rays now shimmering down,
droolings of light shape the contours of his buttocks,
and against a background of gently falling snow,
a shadow crouches, detailed, pink like hollyhock...
—Fantastic, a nose pursues Venus to the clouds.

MAY, 1871

Les poètes de sept ans

Et la Mère, fermant le livre du devoir,
S'en allait satisfaite et très fière, sans voir,
Dans les yeux bleus et sous le front plein d'éminences
L'âme de son enfant livrée aux répugnances.

Tout le jour il suait d'obéissance; très
Intelligent; pourtant des tics noirs, quelques traits,
Semblaient prouver en lui d'âcres hypocrisies.
Dans l'ombre des couloirs aux tentures moisies,
En passant il tirait la langue, les deux poings
À l'aine, et dans ses yeux fermés voyait des points.
Une porte s'ouvrait sur le soir: à la lampe
On le voyait, là-haut, qui râlait sur la rampe,
Sous un golfe de jour pendant du toit. L'été
Surtout, vaincu, stupide, il était entêté
À se renfermer dans la fraîcheur des latrines:
Il pensait là, tranquille et livrant ses narines.
Quand, lavé des odeurs du jour, le jardinet
Derrière la maison, en hiver, s'illunait,
Gisant au pied d'un mur, enterré dans la marne
Et pour des visions écrasant son œil darne,
Il écoutait grouiller les galeux espaliers.
Pitié! ces enfants seuls étaient ses familiers
Qui, chétifs, fronts nus, œil déteignant sur la joue,
Cachant de maigres doigts jaunes et noirs de boue
Sous des habits puant la foire et tout vieillots,
Conversaient avec la douceur des idiots!
Et si, l'ayant surpris à des pitiés immondes,
La mère s'effrayait; les tendresses, profondes,
De l'enfant se jetaient sur cet étonnement.
C'était bon. Elle avait le bleu regard,—qui ment!

À sept ans, il faisait des romans, sur la vie
Du grand désert, où luit la Liberté ravie,

The Poet at Seven Years

And the mother, having shut the exercise book,
departed haughtily, though she dimly mistook
the blue eyes for duty, the brow for repentance
—for the young child's soul seeped oily repugnance.

Supremely intelligent, for that long, dry day
he sweated obedience; yet, some darker strains
spasmed his cheek, advertising his hypocrisy!
In dimly-lit halls decked with mildewed drapery,
his two fists in his groin, his tongue stiff as a dart,
he'd squeeze his eyelids shut, airborne among the spots.
A portal showing onto evening: by the lamps
you would see him, upstairs, grappling with his cramps,
in a gulf of light pouring from the roof. Summers,
especially, conquered, stupid, but yet stubborn
he would shut himself up in the foulest outhouse,
and sit there, tranquil, his nostrils enflamed—aroused.
When, cleansed of the day's stench, the delicate garden
behind the house, snowing, the moon luminescent,
he'd muck in sties of clay piled against a white fence,
squeezing swampy eyes to ornament his visions.
He heard music in the twisting ivy—sixth sense!
And yet, what pity! He could only count as friends
those children who, eyes dripping with putrescence,
sallow, with tattered scarves, would hide their muddy hands
in thin rags reeking of diarrheal events.
They spoke with the smutty gentleness of morons!
And if she caught him in deeds of dark charity,
his mother, scandalized, would summarily receive
his blushing tenderness to assuage her surprise.
All's good. Yes, she could inspire those blue eyes—that lie!

At seven years, he wrote novels brimming with scenes
in epic deserts where, exiled, shone Liberty!

Forêts, soleils, rios, savanes!—Il s'aidait
De journaux illustrés où, rouge, il regardait
Des Espagnoles rire et des Italiennes.
Quand venait, l'œil brun, folle, en robes d'indiennes,
—Huit ans,—la fille des ouvriers d'à côté,
La petite brutale, et qu'elle avait sauté,
Dans un coin, sur son dos, en secouant ses tresses,
Et qu'il était sous elle, il lui mordait les fesses,
Car elle ne portait jamais de pantalons;
—Et, par elle meurtri des poings et des talons,
Remportait les saveurs de sa peau dans sa chambre.

Il craignait les blafards dimanches de décembre,
Où, pommadé, sur un guéridon d'acajou,
Il lisait une Bible à la tranche vert-chou;
Des rêves l'oppressaient chaque nuit dans l'alcôve.
Il n'aimait pas Dieu; mais les hommes, qu'au soir fauve,
Noirs, en blouse, il voyait rentrer dans le faubourg
Où les crieurs, en trois roulements de tambour
Font autour des édits rire et gronder les foules.
—Il rêvait la prairie amoureuse, où des houles
Lumineuses, parfums sains, pubescences d'or,
Font leur remuement calme et prennent leur essor!

Et comme il savourait surtout les sombres choses,
Quand, dans la chambre nue aux persiennes closes,
Haute et bleue, âcrement prise d'humidité,
Il lisait son roman sans cesse médité,
Plein de lourds ciels ocreux et de forêts noyées,
De fleurs de chair aux bois sidérals déployées,
Vertige, écroulements, déroutes et pitié!
—Tandis que se faisait la rumeur du quartier,
En bas,—seul, et couché sur des pièces de toile
Écrue, et pressentant violemment la voile!

26 Mai 1871

Forests, suns, rios and savannas! Then for aid,
he would scan the magazines where, as his pulse raced,
he'd ogle laughing girls, Spanish and Italian.
And when that silly flirt, daughter of the peasants
next door, when she—eight years old!—brown eyes,
in a ripped calico dress, leapt from a corner
mounting him like a horse and shaking her wild curls,
and he was under her, he nipped her derrière
—for the peasants' daughter never donned her panties—
by her her knees, her heels, her claws, he was badly bruised.
He carried the taste of her flesh back to his room.

Little he loathed more than gray, December Sundays,
when, hair pomaded, on a stool of varnished teak,
he'd read from a Bible, its edges cabbage-green.
Dreams harassed him as he tossed in his bare den.
He didn't love God; rather, the laborers, men
he saw each night, tanned, in jackets, lumbering home
to squalid squares with criers who, with thrice-rapped drums,
choked the crowd with edicts puked by elected fools.
He summoned erotic prairies, where shining swells
of natural perfumes lifted gold pubescences
to elevated heights, haloed by innocence.

Since, above all, he savored the contraband stuff,
within his rooms's dry walls, his windows shuttered up,
soaring and blue, with a temper unseasonal,
he reviewed, yet again, his thick loose-leafed novel
scrawled with dense, ocherous skies and sweltering forests,
astral woods brimming with crisply opened flowers,
dizziness, explosions, riots, heroes' marches!
And, as sounds filtered in from the nearby alleys,
he'd lie, alone, on miles of unfurled canvas—still
pure, unbleached—but violently announcing a sail!

MAY 26, 1871

Les pauvres a l'eglise

Parqués entre des bancs de chêne, aux coins d'église
Qu'attiédit puamment leur souffle, tous leurs yeux
Vers le chœur ruisselant d'orrie et la maîtrise
Aux vingt gueules gueulant les cantiques pieux;

Comme un parfum de pain humant l'odeur de cire,
Heureux, humiliés comme des chiens battus,
Les Pauvres au bon Dieu, le patron et le sire,
Tendent leurs oremus risibles et têtus.

Aux femmes, c'est bien bon de faire des bancs lisses,
Après les six jours noirs où Dieu les fait souffrir!
Elles bercent, tordus dans d'étranges pelisses,
Des espèces d'enfants qui pleurent à mourir;

Leurs seins crasseux dehors, ces mangeuses de soupe,
Une prière aux yeux et ne priant jamais,
Regardent parader mauvaisement un groupe
De gamines avec leurs chapeaux déformés

Dehors, le froid, la faim, l'homme en ribote:
C'est bon. Encore une heure; après, les maux sans noms!
—Cependant, alentour, geint, nasille, chuchote
Une collection de vieilles à fanons:

Ces effarés y sont et ces épileptiques
Dont on se détournait hier aux carrefours;
Et, fringalant du nez dans des missels antiques
Ces aveugles qu'un chien introduit dans les cours.

Et tous, bavant la foi mendiante et stupide,
Récitent la complainte infinie à Jésus
Qui rêve en haut, jauni par le vitrail livide,
Loin des maigres mauvais et des méchants pansus,

The Poor in Church

Crowding the church corners, parked in their oaken pens
that their warm breath freshens with reek, their eyes all glued
to the gilt chancel and the choir just above them
with its twenty gaping jaws jawing pious odes—

sniffing, as if aromatic bread, wax odors,
happy, humiliated like whip-beaten curs,
these Poor of the good Lord, their patron and master,
bubble with their risible, but stubborn, prayers.

For women, it feels good to wear the benches smooth
after the six black days when God grants only pain;
they cradle in odd wrappings their one and only boon:
beasts (or are they children?) who wail like they're dying!

Dirty breasts uncovered, these slobberers of soup,
a prayer in their eyes and yet who never pray,
watch, as if a parade, the neighborhood girls group
and preen, gamine models, their hats bent out of shape.

Outside, the cold, the hunger—their men on the town,
drunk again! Oh, well. And in an hour, endless ills.
—Meanwhile, the next pew over: sniffles, whispers, groans,
a catalog of women with loose, dangling chins.

The terrified are here; there, the epileptics
one didn't help yesterday by the dry crossroad;
there, burying their noses in ancient texts,
are the blind whom a dog led into the courtyard.

And all, blubbering a stupid begging of faith,
recite their endless complaints to the Lord Jesus
who dreams above, ensconced in yellow, livid panes
far from wicked stick men and pot-bellied gangsters,

Loin de senteurs de viande et d'étoffes moisies,
Farce prostrée et sombre aux gestes repoussants;
—Et l'oraison fleurit d'expressions choisies,
Et les mysticités prennent des tons pressants,

Quand, des nefs où périt le soleil, plis de soie
Banals, sourires verts, les Dames des quartiers
Distingués,—ô Jésus!—les malades du foie
Font baiser leurs longs doigts jaunes aux bénitiers.

Juin 1871

far from the smells of meat and of moldy garments,
this prostrated farce of loathsome genuflections
—the prayers flower forth into choice expressions
as the mysticities reach imperative tones...

—When, from the naves where the sun chokes, in banal folds
of silk, green smiles, Ladies from the Right Side of Town,
those with sassy servants, wheat allergies—oh Christ!—
dip long yellow fingers in holy-water fonts.

JUNE, 1871

Les premières communions

I.

Vraiment, c'est bête, ces églises des villages
Où quinze laids marmots, encrassant les piliers
Écoutent, grasseyant les divins babillages,
Un noir grotesque dont fermentent les souliers:
Mais le soleil éveille, à travers des feuillages
Les vieilles couleurs des vitraux irréguliers.

La pierre sent toujours la terre maternelle
Vous verrez des monceaux de ces cailloux terreux
Dans la campagne en rut qui frémit solennelle
Portant près des blés lourds, dans les sentiers ocreux,
Ces arbrisseaux brûlés où bleuit la prunelle,
Des nœuds de mûriers noirs et de rosiers fuireux.

Tous les cent ans on rend ces granges respectables
Par un badigeon d'eau bleue et de lait caillé:
Si des mysticités grotesques sont notables
Près de la Notre-Dame ou du Saint empaillé,
Des mouches sentant bon l'auberge et les étables
Se gorgent de cire au plancher ensoleillé.

L'enfant se doit surtout à la maison, famille
Des soins naïfs, des bons travaux abrutissants;
Ils sortent, oubliant que la peau leur fourmille
Où le prêtre du Christ plaqua ses doigts puissants.
On paie au Prêtre un toit ombré d'une charmille
Pour qu'il laisse au soleil tous ces fronts brunissants.

Le premier habit noir, le plus beau jour de tartes
Sous le Napoléon ou le Petit Tambour
Quelque enluminure où les Josephs et les Marthes
Tirent la langue avec un excessif amour
Et que joindront, au jour de science, deux cartes,
Ces seuls doux souvenirs lui restent du grand Jour.

First Communions

I.

Truly, it's stupid, these moldy village churches
where fifteen ugly brats befouling the pillars
bow down to the One babbling the divine nonsense
—a grotesque priest, profound in his reeking sandals.
But the sun returns; it slices through the foliage,
and fires the colors of the misshapen stained glass.

The stone still retains the smell of maternal earth;
you can see small heaps of earth-encrusted pebbles
in the wanton fields as they solemnly quiver
upholding the dense wheat on ocherous rambles,
the burned trees where the plum blues, where black mulberries
and rosebushes grow entwined, spattered with cow shit.

Once a hundred years, these barns are revitalized
with a coat of blue paint, a splash of curdled milk.
If grotesque mysticities are infamous
near Our Lady or the taxidermied Saint, flies,
reeking with the scents of the inn and the stables,
gorge on the hardened wax of the summer-drenched tiles.

The child owes a debt to the home and family,
simple chores—also, their stupefying labors.
They finish, forgetting that their skin teems with burns
where the priest of Christ once laid powerful fingers.
They provide the Priest with a cool grove—but still he
banishes to harsh noon the children's reddened brows.

The first Black Suit, on the finest day of pastries,
under Napoleon or the wee Drummer Boy,
or an old engraving where Josephs and Marthas
stick out their tongues in an excess of old passions,
and which a pair of maps will join in Science Week
—for him, only thoughts of the Great Day will remain.

Les filles vont toujours à l'église, contentes
De s'entendre appeler garces par les garçons
Qui font du genre après messe ou vêpres chantantes.
Eux qui sont destinés au chic des garnisons
Ils narguent au café les maisons importantes
Blousés neuf, et gueulant d'effroyables chansons.

Cependant le Curé choisit pour les enfances
Des dessins; dans son clos, les vêpres dites, quand
L'air s'emplit du lointain nasillement des danses
Il se sent, en dépit des célestes défenses,
Les doigts de pied ravis et le mollet marquant.

—La Nuit vient, noir pirate aux cieux d'or débarquant.

II.

Le Prêtre a distingué parmi les catéchistes,
Congrégés des Faubourgs ou des Riches Quartiers,
Cette petite fille inconnue, aux yeux tristes,
Front jaune. Les parents semblent de doux portiers
"Au grand Jour, le marquant parmi les Catéchistes,
Dieu fera sur ce front neiger ses bénitiers."

III.

La veille du grand Jour, l'enfant se fait malade.
Mieux qu'à l'Église haute aux funèbres rumeurs,
D'abord le frisson vient,—le lit n'étant pas fade—
Un frisson surhumain qui retourne: "Je meurs..."

Et, comme un vol d'amour fait à ses sœurs stupides,
Elle compte, abattue et les mains sur son cœur,
Les Anges, les Jésus et ses Vierges nitides
Et, calmement, son âme a bu tout son vainqueur.

Adonaï!...—Dans les terminaisons latines,
Des cieux moirés de vert baignent les Fronts vermeils

Giddily, girls scramble to the churches, eager
to hear themselves called sluts by the cavorting boys
who strut around after mass or singing vespers.
The boys are destined for the romance of barracks;
in cafés, they jeer at houses of the highborn,
smart in new duds, drawling out horrifying lays.

Meanwhile, the Curé chooses for his young charges
some drawings; in his garden, after vespers, when
the air resounds with nasalities of far off
dances, he feels, despite his holy defenses
his toes delighted, and his calves marking rhythms.

—Night comes, a black pirate climbing to the heavens.

II.

From among the unbaptized converts flowing in
from suburbs and rich quarters, the priest has chosen
a strange little girl—skin sallow, sad demeanor.
Her parents are thrilled like sycophantic porters:
"What a great day! The first pick among the converts!
God's holy fonts…—will snow down on your sallow skin!"

III.

On the eve of the Great Day—the fraught child falls ill!
Like funereal echoes in the church's heights,
first, the shudders arrive—this bed is eventful—
a superhuman shudder that quakes: "Here, I die…"

And, as if stealing love from her stupid sisters,
exhausted, she adds up, one hand over her heart,
the Angels, the Jesuses, the crystal Virgins,
until, calmly, her soul has drunk her Conqueror.

Adonai!—Dizzy in her Latin declensions
where skies swirl with greens that drench the ruddy brows,

Et, tachés du sang pur des célestes poitrines
De grands linges neigeux tombent sur les soleils!

—Pour ses virginités présentes et futures
Elle mord aux fraîcheurs de ta Rémission,
Mais plus que les lys d'eau, plus que les confitures
Tes pardons sont glacés, ô Reine de Sion!

IV.

Puis la Vierge n'est plus que la vierge du livre
Les mystiques élans se cassent quelquefois...
Et vient la pauvreté des images, que cuivre
L'ennui, l'enluminure atroce et les vieux bois;

Des curiosités vaguement impudiques
Épouvantent le rêve aux chastes bleuités
Qui s'est surpris autour des célestes tuniques,
Du linge dont Jésus voile ses nudités.

Elle veut, elle veut, pourtant, l'âme en détresse,
Le front dans l'oreiller creusé par les cris sourds
Prolonger les éclairs suprêmes de tendresse,
Et bave...—L'ombre emplit les maisons et les cours.

Et l'enfant ne peut plus. Elle s'agite, cambre
Les reins et d'une main ouvre le rideau bleu
Pour amener un peu la fraîcheur de la chambre
Sous le drap, vers son ventre et sa poitrine en feu...

V.

Ô son réveil,—minuit,—la fenêtre était blanche.
Devant le sommeil bleu des rideaux illunés,
La vision la prit des candeurs du dimanche,
Elle avait rêvé rouge. Elle saigna du nez.

Et se sentant bien chaste et pleine de faiblesse
Pour savourer en Dieu son amour revenant,

linens of snow descend, dappled with the pure blood
of the celestial breasts, in sun-banishing clouds!

To tend to her chastity, now and forever,
she bites into the coolness of your Remission,
but more than water lilies, more than jams and sweets,
your clemency is frigid—oh Queen of Zion!

IV.

The Virgin is now but a virgin from a book.
At times, her mystical spasms cease, sputtering...
The poverty of images yawns, and boredom
erupts from corny pictures and dumb engravings.

Curiosities—vague, indecent—frighten her,
scandalizing her dreams once colored a chaste blue.
She becomes obsessed with the celestial tunic,
the cloth that keeps Jesus from walking in the nude.

She tries, she tries, now that her soul is so distressed,
to mute her stifled cries, her face in a pillow,
to prolong these crowning orgies of tenderness
—she drools... and darkness buries the houses and courts.

And the child cannot go on. She shifts, she arches
her back, and with one hand retracts the blue curtains
to let in fresh air from the spacious outer yard
that cools the sheets—and her belly and breast that burn!

V.

When she awoke—at midnight!—the window was white.
In front of the blue sleep of the moonlit curtains
visions had besieged her of Sunday's purities.
She had dreamt red. Now, to her surprise, her nose bled.

And feeling very chaste and mortally weakened,
she thirsted for night where, in God, she could feel love,

Elle eut soif de la nuit où s'exalte et s'abaisse
Le cœur, sous l'œil des cieux doux, en les devinant,

De la nuit, Vierge-Mère impalpable, qui baigne
Tous les jeunes émois de ses silences gris;
Elle eut soif de la nuit forte où le cœur qui saigne
Ecoule sans témoin sa révolte sans cris.

Et faisant la Victime et la petite épouse,
Son étoile la vit, une chandelle aux doigts
Descendre dans la cour où séchait une blouse,
Spectre blanc, et lever les spectres noirs des toits...

VI.

Elle passa sa nuit sainte dans les latrines.
Vers la chandelle, aux trous du toit coulait l'air blanc,
Et quelque vigne folle aux noirceurs purpurines,
En deçà d'une cour voisine s'écroulant.

La lucarne faisait un cœur de lueur vive
Dans la cour où les cieux bas plaquaient d'ors vermeils
Les vitres; les pavés puant l'eau de lessive
Soufraient l'ombre des murs bondés de noirs sommeils.

VII.

Qui dira ces langueurs et ces pitiés immondes,
Et ce qu'il lui viendra de haine, ô sales fous
Dont le travail divin déforme encor les mondes,
Quand la lèpre à la fin mangera ce corps doux?
....

VIII.

Et quand, ayant rentré tous ses nœuds d'hystéries,
Elle verra, sous les tristesses du bonheur,
L'amant rêver au blanc million des Maries,
Au matin de la nuit d'amour avec douleur:

heart rising and falling for the eyes of heaven
as it felt their presence returning, white and soft.

For night, impalpable Virgin-Mother, that bathes
all the young emotions with its silver silence—
she thirsted for the strong night where her bleeding heart
could mutely caterwaul, its revolt unwitnessed.

And acting both the Victim and devoted Spouse,
she went, candle in hand, watched by her only star,
down into the courtyard where a flapping coat dried,
—she, a white specter, called black specters from the tiles.

VI.

She spent her Holy Night hidden in the outhouse.
Through holes in the roof, white air pricked at her candle;
nearby, a maddened vine of blackish purple hue
pitifully dropped from walls beside the stables.

The skylight shimmered like a nimble heart aglow;
the pavement smelled of wash water; in the courtyard,
low-hanging clouds dyed the window panes reddish gold
—shadows filled with black sleep flooded from narrow walls.

VII.

The hate that flows into her—oh prurient clowns
whose divine efforts still decimate our worlds!—who
will speak of the languors, the squalid pity, when
leprosy, in the end, consumes this sweet body?
....

VIII.

And when, after the knots of hysteria ceased,
she sees, under the melancholies of happiness,
her lover dreaming of a million white Marys,
on the morning of the night of love, with sadness:

"Sais-tu que je t'ai fait mourir? J'ai pris ta bouche,
Ton cœur, tout ce qu'on a, tout ce que vous avez;
Et moi, je suis malade: Oh! je veux qu'on me couche
Parmi les Morts des eaux nocturnes abreuvés

"J'étais bien jeune, et Christ a souillé mes haleines
Il me bonda jusqu'à la gorge de dégoûts!
Tu baisais mes cheveux profonds comme les laines
Et je me laissais faire... ah! va, c'est bon pour vous,

"Hommes! qui songez peu que la plus amoureuse
Est, sous sa conscience aux ignobles terreurs,
La plus prostituée et la plus douloureuse,
Et que tous nos élans vers Vous sont des erreurs!

"Car ma Communion première est bien passée.
Tes baisers, je ne puis jamais les avoir sus:
Et mon cœur et ma chair par ta chair embrassée
Fourmillent du baiser putride de Jésus!"

IX.

Alors l'âme pourrie et l'âme désolée
Sentiront ruisseler tes malédictions
—Ils auront couché sur ta Haine inviolée,
Échappés, pour la mort, des justes passions.

Christ! ô Christ, éternel voleur des énergies
Dieu qui pour deux mille ans vouas à ta pâleur
Cloués au sol, de honte et de céphalalgies
Ou renversés les fronts des femmes de douleur.

Juillet 1871

"Do you know I caused your death? That I took your mouth,
your heart, all that you are, everything that you own.
And I—I am sick. Oh, please lay me down among
the Dead who have nursed on the midnight's dark ocean!

"I was very young, and Christ corrupted my breath.
He stuffed me to the gills with measureless disgust!
You laid kisses on my hair, once as thick as wool,
—and I permitted it... Well! you do as you must...

you Men! You don't care that the girl most in love
is, with her consciousness of ignoble terrors,
the most prostituted and the most remorseful,
—that our passions for You are repulsive errors!

For my First Communion is now over. Never
could I have acknowledged the worth of your kisses.
Now, my heart and my flesh set aflame by your flesh,
reek to the core with the putrid kiss of Jesus!"

IX.

Now, the filthy soul, distressed spirit, will feel your
maledictions, your curses, upon their low heads.
—They will have lain down with your inviolate Hate
and, in lieu of just passions, will choose their own death.

Christ! Oh, Christ! eternal sapper of energies,
who entrapped with your pallor for two thousand years
—nailed them to the ground with shame and cephalagies,
or tossed them backward—the brows of sorrowful girls!

JULY, 1871

L'Homme juste

[...]

Le Juste restait droit sur ses hanches solides:
Un rayon lui dorait l'épaule; des sueurs
Me prirent: "Tu veux voir rutiler les bolides?
Et, debout, écouter bourdonner les fleurs
D'astres lactés, et les essaims d'astéroïdes?

"Par des farces de nuit ton front est épié,
Ô juste! Il faut gagner un toit. Dis ta prière,
La bouche dans ton drap doucement expié;
Et si quelque égaré choque ton ostiaire,
Dis: Frère, va plus loin, je suis estropié!"

Et le Juste restait debout, dans l'épouvante
Bleuâtre des gazons après le soleil mort:
"Alors, mettrais-tu tes genouillères en vente,
Ô vieillard? Pèlerin sacré! Barde d'Armor!
Pleureur des Oliviers! Main que la pitié gante!

"Barbe de la famille et poing de la cité,
Croyant très doux: ô cœur tombé dans les calices,
Majestés et vertus, amour et cécité,
Juste! plus bête et plus dégoûtant que les lices!
Je suis celui qui souffre et qui s'est révolté!

"Et ça me fait pleurer sur mon ventre, ô stupide,
Et bien rire, l'espoir fameux de ton pardon!
Je suis maudit, tu sais! Je suis soûl, fou, livide,
Ce que tu veux! Mais va te coucher, voyons donc,
Juste! Je ne veux rien à ton cerveau torpide!

"C'est toi le Juste, enfin, le Juste! C'est assez!
C'est vrai que ta tendresse et ta raison sereines

The Just Man

[...]

The Just Man stood before me on solid haunches,
a ray of light gilding his shoulder. I began
to sweat. "Do you want to see flaming rockets? Or,
sublimely tall, to hear the drones of influence
from the nacreous stars, the swarms of asteroids?

"During your night farces, your forehead spied upon,
—oh Just Man!—you seek a roof, you say a prayer,
your mouth buried in sheets to mute your atonements.
And if some indigent falls upon your old bones,
you shout: 'Brother, leave me! You see—I am broken!'"

The Just Man floated there, still, in the bluish dark
horror of lawns after the suicides of suns.
"Weeper of olive trees! Pity gloving your hand!
Old man, would you put your kneecaps up for auction?
You, Holy Pilgrim! You, Bard of Armorica!

"Beard of the family—but fist of the city—
heart toppled over into chalices with love
and blindness, majesties and virtues—oh princely
believer! Just Man! More repulsive than mastiffs!
I am the one who suffers—who revolted here!

"You, idiot, make me weep into my belly
and laugh—the famous 'deliverance' of your pardon!
I am cursed, you know. I am drunk, livid, insane
—whatever you think! Really, stand down—yes? Just Man,
I mean it! I want nothing of your addled brain!

"You are the Just Man—great! You are the Just Man—swell!
It's true that your reason and cool tenderness weave

Reniflent dans la nuit comme des cétacés!
Que tu te fais proscrire, et dégoises des thrènes
Sur d'effroyables becs de canne fracassés!

"Et c'est toi l'œil de Dieu! le lâche! quand les plantes
Froides des pieds divins passeraient sur mon cou,
Tu es lâche! Ô ton front qui fourmille de lentes!
Socrates et Jésus, Saints et Justes, dégoût!
Respectez le Maudit suprême aux nuits sanglantes!"

J'avais crié cela sur la terre, et la nuit
Calme et blanche occupait les Cieux pendant ma fièvre
Je relevai mon front: le fantôme avait fui,
Emportant l'ironie atroce de ma lèvre...
—Vents nocturnes, venez au Maudit! Parlez-lui!

Cependant que, silencieux sous les pilastres
D'azur, allongeant les comètes et les nœuds
D'univers, remuement énorme sans désastres,
L'ordre, éternel veilleur, rame aux cieux lumineux
Et de sa drague en feu laisse filer les astres!

Ah! qu'il s'en aille, lui, la gorge cravatée
De honte, ruminant toujours mon ennui, doux
Comme le sucre sur la denture gâtée
—Tel que la chienne après l'assaut des fiers toutous,
Léchant son flanc d'où pend une entraille emportée

Qu'il dise charités crasseuses et progrès...
—J'exècre tous ces yeux de Chinois [ou d]aines,
[Mais] qui chante: nana, comme un tas d'enfants près
De mourir, idiots doux aux chansons soudaines:
Ô Justes, nous chierons dans vos ventres de grès

through the air like a gray whale, and that you have made
yourself quite an exile, that you howl threnodies
over terrible, crushed-into-pieces duck bills!

"But then you are the eye of God? You coward! Might
the divine feet's icy soles stamp upon my neck,
you'd only laugh! Oh, with your brow crawling with lice!
Socrates? Jesus? Saintly and wise? Pathetic!
Look! I am the supreme Accurséd of bleeding night!"

I howled this over the earth, and peaceful and white,
during my long fever, the evening filled the skies.
I raised my head. I saw the ghost had calmly fled,
taking with him the dark ironies from my lips!
—Night winds, come to this curséd man! —Speak to him!

—Meanwhile, silently, under the blue pilasters,
swift-passing comets and clusters of galaxies,
—a manic bustling, whirring without disasters—
Order, the Eternal Watchman, steered through the skies,
luminous stars shooting from his flaming dragnet!

Ah, let him go off, his neck tethered by a tie
of shame, still ruminating on my boredom, sweet
as sugar festering in the rot of bad teeth,
or, like a bitch after assaults from rabid dogs
who licks her bloody flanks from which her entrails seep!

Enough with all this dirty Charity! Progress!
I'm sick of all the Chinese eyes, all the smugness
that sings Na Na Na! like from the mouths of urchins
approaching death—sweet idiots with their bright songs!
—Yes, Just Man! We will shit in your bellies of stone!

1871

Les assis

Noirs de loupes, grêlés, les yeux cerclés de bagues
Vertes, leurs doigts boulus crispés à leurs fémurs,
Le sinciput plaqué de hargnosités vagues
Comme les floraisons lépreuses des vieux murs;

Ils ont greffé dans des amours épileptiques
Leur fantasque ossature aux grands squelettes noirs
De leurs chaises; leurs pieds aux barreaux rachitiques
S'entrelacent pour les matins et pour les soirs!

Ces vieillards ont toujours fait tresse avec leurs sièges,
Sentant les soleils vifs percaliser leur peau,
Ou, les yeux à la vitre où se fanent les neiges,
Tremblant du tremblement douloureux du crapaud.

Et les Sièges leur ont des bontés: culottée
De brun, la paille cède aux angles de leurs reins;
L'âme des vieux soleils s'allume emmaillotée
Dans ces tresses d'épis où fermentaient les grains.

Et les Assis, genoux aux dents, verts pianistes
Les dix doigts sous leur siège aux rumeurs de tambour
S'écoutent clapoter des barcarolles tristes,
Et leurs caboches vont dans des roulis d'amour.

—Oh! ne les faites pas lever! C'est le naufrage...
Ils surgissent, grondant comme des chats giflés,
Ouvrant lentement leurs omoplates, ô rage!
Tout leur pantalon bouffe à leurs reins boursouflés.

Et vous les écoutez, cognant leurs têtes chauves
Aux murs sombres, plaquant et plaquant leurs pieds tors
Et leurs boutons d'habit sont des prunelles fauves
Qui vous accrochent l'œil du fond des corridors!

The Sitting Men

With blackened cysts, pock-marked, and eyes tugged at by green
bags, swollen fingers clenched around skeletal thighs,
their haughty pates mottled by thin, delicate strands
like the leprous ivy of walls claiming the sky

—For hours, orgasming in epileptic amours
with their chairs, their bones grafted to the varnished forms,
their legs entwined like snakes around stripped, withered trunks,
sinning, day and night, in rank, Edenic coverts.

Feeling the hot sun make burlap of their skin, these
men insist—that they will never abort their seats!
Or, with eyes to casement windows, bemoaning snows,
they shake—sportively—like electrocuted toads.

And the seats are good to them: the dark brown caning
droops to the eely shape of their anemic hinds;
the souls of ancient suns rise, illuminating
within their hairs' weaves a virile fermentation.

And these seated men, knees in teeth, green pianists,
their ten fingers hammering, like a tambourine,
the crackling straw—pulse of a sad barcarole!—bliss
marring their faces as they rock, in love, again.

—Oh, don't make them stand up! Ugh! What a shipwreck!
but lo, they get up... growling like scolded cats, stiff
as paper skeletons; as their tender blades flex,
their pants balloon around their Olympian limbs.

And you can hear them knock, knocking their bald heads
against the dark walls, stamp, stamping their mangled toes,
—Their jacket buttons? the starved pupils of beasts
leering, skulking, down the wet, salty corridors.

Puis ils ont une main invisible qui tue:
Au retour leur regard filtre ce venin noir
Qui charge l'œil souffrant de la chienne battue
Et vous suez pris dans un atroce entonnoir.

Rassis, les poings noyés dans des manchettes sales
Ils songent à ceux-là qui les ont fait lever
Et, de l'aurore au soir, des grappes d'amygdales
Sous leurs mentons chétifs s'agitent à crever

Quand l'austère sommeil a baissé leurs visières
Ils rêvent sur leur bras de sièges féconds,
De vrais petits amours de chaises en lisière
Par lesquelles de fiers bureaux seront bordés;

Des fleurs d'encre crachant des pollens en virgule
Les bercent, le long des calices accroupis
Tels qu'au fil des glaïeuls le vol des libellules
—Et leur membre s'agace à des barbes d'épis.

Suddenly, they have that magic hand—that murders!
Returning, their eyes sift the air for black toxins
miming the pleading eye of a flea-gored bitch, so
you sweat. You are squeezed down execrable funnels.

Relieved, rethroned, their wrists ringed again by stained cuffs,
they pause, they ponder, ask: who called for exercise?
—And again, from mornings to nights, their tonsils bunched
in miniature chins, they squint for fratricides.

And when a stately sleep finally slams their eyes,
they screen pornographic dreams: seductive chairs...
—pregnant chairs! bureaus that pump out pink, chubby stools—
so proud, macho, of the generations they sire!

Flowers of ink spit out their pollen in commas,
and comfort them... the rows of drooping calyxes,
flights of dragonflies through files of gladiolas
—and the barbed ears of corn arouse their penises.

1870-1872

5: THE SEER

It is about reaching the unknown by the disordering of *all the senses*. The sufferings are enormous, but one has to be strong, have been born a poet, and I know I am a poet. This is not my fault at all. It is wrong to say: I think. One ought to say: I am being thought.

—Rimbaud to Georges Izambard, May 13, 1871

Le cœur volé

Mon triste cœur bave à la poupe,
Mon cœur couvert de caporal:
Ils y lancent des jets de soupe,
Mon triste cœur bave à la poupe:
Sous les quolibets de la troupe
Qui pousse un rire général,
Mon triste cœur bave à la poupe,
Mon cœur couvert de caporal!

Ithyphalliques et pioupiesques
Leurs quolibets l'ont dépravé!
Au gouvernail on voit des fresques
Ithyphalliques et pioupiesques
Ô flots abracadabrantesques
Prenez mon cœur, qu'il soit lavé:
Ithyphalliques et pioupiesques
Leurs quolibets l'ont dépravé!

Quand ils auront tari leurs chiques
Comment agir, ô cœur volé?
Ce seront des refrains bachiques
Quand ils auront tari leurs chiques
J'aurai des sursauts stomachiques
Moi, si mon cœur est ravalé:
Quand ils auront tari leurs chiques
Comment agir, ô cœur volé?

Mai 1871

The Stolen Heart

My sad heart dribbles on the deck,
my heart slick with tobacco spit.
As they spit streams of soup at it,
my sad heart dribbles on the deck.
Tossed by jeers of a rangy troop
who laugh and writhe—oh what a coup!—
my sad heart dribbles on the deck,
my heart slick with tobacco spit.

Ithyphallic and soldieresque,
their scoffing stuns and depraves it.
You see the walls: cartoons they sketch,
ithyphallic and soldieresque.
Oh abracadabraic waves,
restore my heart, let it be saved!
Ithyphallic and soldieresque,
their scoffing stuns and depraves it.

When they have used up all their chaw,
my stolen heart—can I survive?
Their Bacchic belches start to rise,
when they have used up all their chaw.
I'll have a belly ache and retch,
my heart dismissed, an excrement.
When they have used up all their chaw,
my stolen heart—can I survive?

1871

Mes petites amoureuses

Un hydrolat lacrymal lave
    Les cieux vert-chou:
Sous l'arbre tendronnier qui bave,
    Vos caoutchoucs

Blancs de lunes particulières
    Aux pialats ronds,
Entrechoquez vos genouillères
    Mes laiderons!

Nous nous aimions à cette époque,
    Bleu laideron!
On mangeait des œufs à la coque
    Et du mouron!

Un soir, tu me sacras poète,
    Blond laideron:
Descends ici, que je te fouette
    En mon giron;

J'ai dégueulé ta bandoline,
    Noir laideron;
Tu couperais ma mandoline
    Au fil du front

Pouah! mes salives desséchées,
    Roux laideron
Infectent encor les tranchées
    De ton sein rond!

Ô mes petites amoureuses,
    Que je vous hais!
Plaquez de fouffes douloureuses
    Vos tétons laids!

My Little Lovers

A lacrymal tincture cleanses
   cabbage-green clouds;
beneath the saplings' salivas,
   your wet ponchos...

White with moons quite peculiar,
   round eye organs,
—rattle your kneecaps together,
   my ugly ones!

We loved one another those days,
   blue ugly one!
we ate soft boiled eggs, mayonnaise
   and tarragon!

One night, you dubbed me a poet,
   blond ugly one;
bend down here, receive your torment
   and make a din!

I vomited your brilliantine,
   black ugly one;
you would prune my mandolin
   on my brow line.

Bah! my spit, evaporated,
   foul ginger one,
still infects the deep, winding trench
   of your round bust!

Oh, my many little lovers,
   how I hate you!
renovate with painful blisters
   your ugly dugs!

Piétinez mes vieilles terrines
    De sentiment;
—Hop donc! soyez-moi ballerines
    Pour un moment!...

Vos omoplates se déboîtent,
    Ô mes amours!
Une étoile à vos reins qui boitent,
    Tournez vos tours!

Et c'est pourtant pour ces éclanches
    Que j'ai rimé!
Je voudrais vous casser les hanches
    D'avoir aimé!

Fade amas d'étoiles ratées,
    Comblez les coins!
—Vous crèverez en Dieu, bâtées
    D'ignobles soins!

Sous les lunes particulières
    Aux pialats ronds,
Entrechoquez vos genouillères,
    Mes laiderons!

Trample upon my old basins
 of sentiment
—up now! and be ballerinas
 for one moment!

Your shoulder blades are out of joint,
 oh my lovelies!
a star that limps upon your loins
 weaves as you weave!

And yet, it's for these mutton shoulders
 that I make rhymes!
I would like to bust your haunches
 for these desires!

Worthless piles of aborted stars
 fill the corners!
—you will return to God, ensnared
 by stupid cares!

Under moons quite peculiar,
 round eye organs,
—rattle your kneecaps together,
 my ugly ones!

MAY 15, 1871

Les sœurs de charité

Le jeune homme dont l'œil est brillant, la peau brune,
Le beau corps de vingt ans qui devrait aller nu,
Et qu'eût, le front cerclé de cuivre, sous la lune
Adoré, dans la Perse un Génie inconnu,

Impétueux avec des douceurs virginales
Et noires, fier de ses premiers entêtements,
Pareil aux jeunes mers, pleurs de nuits estivales
Qui se retournent sur des lits de diamants;

Le jeune homme, devant les laideurs de ce monde
Tressaille dans son cœur largement irrité,
Et plein de la blessure éternelle et profonde,
Se prend à désirer sa sœur de charité.

Mais, ô Femme, monceau d'entrailles, pitié douce,
Tu n'es jamais la Sœur de charité, jamais,
Ni regard noir, ni ventre où dort une ombre rousse
Ni doigts légers, ni seins splendidement formés.

Aveugle irréveillée aux immenses prunelles
Tout notre embrassement n'est qu'une question:
C'est toi qui pends à nous, porteuse de mamelles;
Nous te berçons, charmante et grave Passion.

Tes haines, tes torpeurs fixes, tes défaillances,
Et les brutalités souffertes autrefois,
Tu nous rends tout, ô Nuit pourtant sans malveillances,
Comme un excès de sang épanché tous les mois

—Quand la femme, portée un instant, l'épouvante,
Amour appel de vie et chanson d'action
Viennent la Muse verte et la Justice ardente
Le déchirer de leur auguste obsession.

The Sisters of Charity

This young man with brown skin, with a scintillant eye
and comely torso—just twenty!—brow haloed gold
who should go nude, who should stretch under the twilight
worshipped by a Genie in far off Xanadus.

Wild, but sensitive, dark, and slightly arrogant
not subtly impressed by his first rash commands
like juvenescent seas, a summer night's plaint,
tears cried out in diamonds on pillow-swollen beds.

This young man, now faced with the vulgar, dirty world
recoils in his heart, wakes his dormant pity,
suffused with the fire of eternal inner wounds,
he calls to come in—his Sister of Charity.

But, oh Woman, moist heap of viscera, oh sweet
pity! you—you are not the Sister of Charity,
not the dark glance, not the belly where humors sleep,
not the lithe fingers, not the breasts of shapely ivory.

Unawakened blind Woman, your irises wide,
all our dalliance is nothing but a question,
—it's you who swing from us with your pendulous bust;
we rock and swaddle you, grave, charming Passion.

Your failures, your hates, your ossified languors,
your traumas, your lacks, your annals of lost triumphs,
this you give to us, oh night of simple valors,
like the trickle of blood you offer every month.

—When Woman, in the throes of Right, frightens him,
Love, the call of life, the clarion of action,
the emerald Muse and passionate Justice come
to decimate him with venerable obsessions.

Ah! sans cesse altéré des splendeurs et des calmes,
Délaissé des deux Sœurs implacables, geignant
Avec tendresse après la science aux bras almes
Il porte à la nature en fleur son front saignant.

Mais la noire alchimie et les saintes études
Répugnent au blessé, sombre savant d'orgueil;
Il sent marcher sur lui d'atroces solitudes
Alors, et toujours beau, sans dégoût du cercueil,

Qu'il croie aux vastes fins, Rêves ou Promenades
Immenses, à travers les nuits de Vérité,
Et t'appelle en son âme et ses membres malades
Ô Mort mystérieuse, ô sœur de charité!

Juin 1871

Endlessly thirsting for serenity and calm,
moaning, abandoned by these intractable
sisters! reaching out for Science with friendly arms,
he brings to fruition his bleeding, bashed in skull.

Alchemical studies and apocryphal tomes
repulse this savaged man, this dour scholar of pride;
he sees, unfurling forth, a solace like the tomb.
But, yet handsome, with no stance against suicide...

Let him embark into journeys ripe as his dreams,
to trek through nights of Truth, his splendid Narrative!
Oh let him call you with his pale and sickly limbs!
Oh mysterious Death! Sister of Charity!

JUNE, 1871

Voyelles

A noir, E blanc, I rouge, U vert, O bleu: voyelles,
Je dirai quelque jour vos naissances latentes:
A, noir corset velu des mouches éclatantes
Qui bombinent autour des puanteurs cruelles,

Golfes d'ombre; E, candeurs des vapeurs et des tentes,
Lances des glaciers fiers, rois blancs, frissons d'ombelles;
I, pourpres, sang craché, rire des lèvres belles
Dans la colère ou les ivresses pénitentes;

U, cycles, vibrements divins des mers virides,
Paix des pâtis semés d'animaux, paix des rides
Que l'alchimie imprime aux grands fronts studieux;

O, Suprême Clairon plein des strideurs étranges,
Silences traversés des Mondes et des Anges:
—O l'Oméga, rayon violet de Ses Yeux!

Vowels

A black, E white, I red, U green, O blue: vowels,
some day I will betray your burgeoning naissance;
A, a hairy corset of black glittering flies
gamboling around the void of a punishing stench,

gulfs of shadows; E, white of steam clouds, bivouacked tents,
the pikes of proud glaciers, white kings, or Queen Anne's lace;
I, purples, blood from split lips, laughing with vengeance
or saturnine remorse, rouging a doll-like face;

U, circuits, changing tides on divine, green-flecked seas,
peace of dull animals on fertile pastures, peace
of a pensive, curled brow engrossed by Alchemy;

O, Supreme Trumpet, strange with solar key changes,
silences only spanned by Worlds and by Angels,
—O—the Omega—the violet beam from His Eyes!

1870-1872

Ce qu'on dit au poète a propos de fleurs

À Monsieur Théodore de Banville

I.

Ainsi, toujours, vers l'azur noir
Où tremble la mer des topazes,
Fonctionneront dans ton soir
Les Lys, ces clystères d'extases!

À notre époque de sagous
Quand les Plantes sont travailleuses,
Le Lys boira les bleus dégoûts
Dans tes Proses religieuses!

—Le lys de monsieur de Kerdrel
Le Sonnet de mil huit cent trente,
Le Lys qu'on donne au Ménestrel
Avec l'œillet et l'amarante!

Des lys! Des lys! On n'en voit pas!
Et dans ton Vers, tel que les manches
Des Pécheresses aux doux pas,
Toujours frissonnent ces fleurs blanches!

Toujours, Cher, quand tu prends un bain,
Ta chemise aux aisselles blondes
Se gonfle aux brises du matin
Sur les myosotis immondes!

L'amour ne passe à tes octrois
Que les Lilas,—à balançoires!
Et les Violettes du Bois,
Crachats sucrés des Nymphes noires!...

What Is Said to the Poet Concerning Flowers

To Monsieur Théodore de Banville

I.

Yes, always, toward the black azure
where seas of topazes shimmer,
able Lilies—those pessaries
of ecstasy!—will serve your night.

In our own epoch of sago
when Plants are dutiful workers,
the Lily will suck blue loathing
from out your religious Proses!

—Monsieur de Kerdrel's fleur-de-lys,
The Sonnet of 1830,
the Lily slipped to a Minstrel
with the amaranth and the pink!

Lilies! Lilies! Not one to pick!
But in your Verse, like the sleeves of
Women of Sin who step softly,
always, these white flowers shiver!

Each time, my Dear Sir, that you bathe,
your shirt with yellow armpits
swells in the morning breeze above
the appalling forget-me-nots!

Love lets nothing past your roadblocks
but Lilacs—oh, the fickleness!—
and the violets of the forest?
sugary spittle of black Nymphs!

II.

Ô Poètes, quand vous auriez
Les Roses, les Roses soufflées,
Rouges sur tiges de lauriers,
Et de mille octaves enflées!

Quand *Banville* en ferait neiger
Sanguinolentes, tournoyantes,
Pochant l'œil fou de l'étranger
Aux lectures mal bienveillantes!

De vos forêts et de vos prés,
Ô très paisibles photographes!
La Flore est diverse à peu près
Comme des bouchons de carafes!

Toujours les végétaux Français,
Hargneux, phtisiques, ridicules,
Où le ventre des chiens bassets
Navigue en paix, aux crépuscules;

Toujours, après d'affreux desseins
De Lotos bleus ou d'Hélianthes,
Estampes roses, sujets saints
Pour de jeunes communiantes!

L'Ode Açoka cadre avec la
Strophe en fenêtre de lorette;
Et de lourds papillons d'éclat
Fientent sur la Pâquerette.

Vieilles verdures, vieux galons!
Ô croquignoles végétales!
Fleurs fantasques des vieux Salons!
—Aux hannetons, pas aux crotales,

II.

Oh Poets, if you had Roses,
Roses, Roses, spun round by wind,
red upon the stems of laurels,
swollen with your eight-line stanzas!

If *Banville* would make them snow down,
blood-tinted and gadding about,
bruising the leer of the stranger
with his base interpretations!

About your forests and meadows,
oh somnolent photographers,
the Flora is just as diverse
as the corks of wine decanters!

Always those French vegetables,
fierce, phthisical, ridiculous,
where the bellies of basset hounds
wander in the twilight at peace.

And afterwards: the bad designs
—the blue Lotuses or Sunflowers,
pink engravings, subjects holy
for girls making First Communion!

The Ode of Asaka works well,
verse like a courtesan's window,
as butterflies, bright and heavy,
are dunging upon the Daisy.

Old perennials, old galloons!
Oh vegetable croqueted biscuits!
Arcane flowers of quaint old dens!
—For cockchafers, not pit vipers,

Ces poupards végétaux en pleurs
Que Grandville eût mis aux lisières,
Et qu'allaitèrent de couleurs
De méchants astres à visières!

Oui, vos bavures de pipeaux
Font de précieuses glucoses!
—Tas d'œufs frits dans de vieux chapeaux,
Lys, Açokas, Lilas et Roses!...

III.

O blanc Chasseur, qui cours sans bas
A travers le Pâtis panique,
Ne peux-tu pas, ne dois-tu pas
Connaître un peu ta botanique?

Tu ferais succéder, je crains,
Aux Grillons roux les Cantharides,
L'or des Rios au bleu des Rhins,
Bref, aux Norwèges les Florides:

Mais, Cher, l'An n'est plus, maintenant,
—C'est la vérité,—de permettre
À l'Eucalyptus étonnant
Des constrictors d'un hexamètre;

Là!... Comme si les Acajous
Ne servaient, même en nos Guyanes,
Qu'aux cascades des sapajous,
Au lourd délire des lianes!

—En somme, une Fleur, Romarin
Ou Lys, vive ou morte, vaut-elle
Un excrément d'oiseau marin?
Vaut-elle un seul pleur de chandelle?

are those vegetable dolls sniveling
that Grandville scrawls on the edges
and, suckling them for colors,
the obnoxious stars with vizors!

Yes, your drooling from shepherd's pipes
creates some precious sugar coats!
—Pile of fried eggs in rheumy hats,
Lilies, Asokas and Roses!...

III.

Oh white Hunter, running barefoot
across the Pastures of panic,
couldn't you not, or ought you not,
know your botany a slight bit?

You would make succeed, I fear, the
Cantharides to russet Crickets,
the gold of Rios to Rhine's
blues—Floridas to Norways.

But, Sir, Art doth not consist now
—this is the truth—in permitting
the astounding Eucalyptus
a boa hexameters long!

You see, Mahogany serves as
something, within our Guyanas,
more than swing sets for monkeys in
deliria of lianas!

—In short, is a Flower, Lily
or Rosemary, dead or alive,
worth the ordure of one seabird?
Worth one wax tear of a candle?

—Et j'ai dit ce que je voulais!
Toi, même assis là-bas, dans une
Cabane de bambous,—volets
Clos, tentures de perse brune,—

Tu torcherais des floraisons
Dignes d'oises extravagantes!...
—Poète! ce sont des raisons
Non moins risibles qu'arrogantes!...

IV.

Dis, non les pampas printaniers
Noirs d'épouvantables révoltes,
Mais les tabacs, les cotonniers!
Dis les exotiques récoltes!

Dis, front blanc que Phébus tanna,
De combien de dollars se rente
Pedro Velasquez, Habana;
Incague la mer de Sorrente

Où vont les Cygnes par milliers;
Que tes strophes soient des réclames
Pous l'abatis des mangliers
Fouillés des hydres et des lames!

Ton quatrain plonge aux bois sanglants
Et revient proposer aux Hommes
Divers sujets de sucres blancs,
De pectoraires et de gommes!

Sachons par Toi si les blondeurs
Des Pics neigeux, vers les Tropiques,
Sont ou des insectes pondeurs
Ou des lichens microscopiques!

—There, I have aired my opinions!
You, sitting over there, in a
Bamboo hut with the shutters closed
and brown Persian rugs for curtains,

even then you'd churn out blossoms
worthy of gaudy Oises!
—Poet! this is your aesthetic,
no less silly than arrogant!

IV.

Speak not of the springtime pampas
black with terrifying revolts,
but of tobacco and cotton
trees—speak of exotic harvests!

Say, white face tanned by Phoebus, how
much cash Pedro Velasquez
in Havana earned in a year;
—excrete on the sea of Sorrento

where Swans travel in the thousands!
Let your verses advocate for
the clearing of mangrove swamplands
that the wave and hydra devour!

Your quatrains plunge into bloody
thickets, then return, offering
to Humanity vast subjects:
white sugar, cough drops, and rubber!

Through You, let us know if the beige
on snowy peaks near the Tropics
are insects laying many eggs
or lichens submicroscopic!

Trouve, ô Chasseur, nous le voulons,
Quelques garances parfumées
Que la Nature en pantalons
Fasse éclore!—pour nos Armées!

Trouve, aux abords du Bois qui dort,
Les fleurs, pareilles à des mufles,
D'où bavent des pommades d'or
Sur les cheveux sombres des Buffles!

Trouve, aux prés fous, où sur le Bleu
Tremble l'argent des pubescences,
Des Calices pleins d'œufs de feu
Qui cuisent parmi les essences!

Trouve des Chardons cotonneux
Dont dix ânes aux yeux de braises
Travaillent à filer les nœuds!
Trouve des Fleurs qui soient des chaises!

Oui, trouve au cœur des noirs filons
Des fleurs presque pierres,—fameuses!—
Qui vers leurs durs ovaires blonds
Aient des amygdales gemmeuses!

Sers-nous, à Farceur, tu le peux,
Sur un plat de vermeil splendide
Des ragoûts de Lys sirupeux
Mordant nos cuillers Alfénide!

V.

Quelqu'un dira le grand Amour,
Voleur des Sombres Indulgences:
Mais ni Renan, ni le chat Murr
N'ont vu les Bleus Thyrses immenses!

Find, oh Hunter, we require it,
a few aromatic madders
that Nature, for our battalions,
causes to blossom as trousers!

Find, just outside the dozing Wood,
the flowers that look like muzzles
from which dribble golden pomades
onto the manes of buffaloes!

Find, in mad fields, where, on the Blue,
silvery pubescence trembles,
calyxes full of fiery eggs
that simmer in essential oils!

Find cottony Thistle fields whose
wool ten donkeys with burning eyes
endeavor to unknot and smooth!
Find the Blossoms that are armchairs!

Yes, in the heart of crevices,
find Flowers almost stones—stunning!—
that have diamantine tonsils
close to their hard blonde ovaries.

Serve us, oh Clown, this you can do,
on a splendid vermilion plate
syrupy Lilyesque ragouts
that rot our Alfénided spoons!

V.

Someone will speak about great Love,
thief of Black Indulgences:
but not Renan, not the cat Murr,
have seen the huge Blue Thyrsuses!

Toi, fais jouer dans nos torpeurs,
Par les parfums les hystéries;
Exalte-nous vers des candeurs
Plus candides que les Maries...

Commerçant! colon! médium!
Ta Rime sourdra, rose ou blanche,
Comme un rayon de sodium,
Comme un caoutchouc qui s'épanche!

De tes noirs Poèmes,—Jongleur!
Blancs, verts, et rouges dioptriques,
Que s'évadent d'étranges fleurs
Et des papillons électriques!

Voilà! c'est le Siècle d'enfer!
Et les poteaux télégraphiques
Vont orner,—lyre aux chants de fer,
Tes omoplates magnifiques!

Surtout, rime une version
Sur le mal des pommes de terre!
—Et, pour la composition
De Poèmes pleins de mystère

Qu'on doive lire de Tréguier
À Paramaribo, rachète
Des Tomes de Monsieur Figuier,
—Illustrés!—chez Monsieur Hachette!

    Alcide Bava
    A. R.

    14 juillet 1871

Make playful in our languors, You,
hysterias with your odors;
exalt us toward the pure whiteness
more pure than that of the Marys...

Tradesman! Colonist! Medium!
your Rhyme, pink or white, will well up
like a glimmer of sodium,
like a rubber tree that's been tapped!

From your ink-black Poems—Juggler!—
through red, green and white dioptics,
allow all bizarre flowers to
burst, and electric butterflies!

You see! it is the Century
of hell! And the telegraph poles
will embellish—iron-voiced lyre—
your magnificent shoulder blades!

But most, rhyme us a rendition
of the last potato famine!
—And, toward the composition
of your mysterious Poems

that are to be read from Tréguier
to Paramaribo, go get
some Volumes by Monsieur Figuier
—well illustrated!—at Hachette's!

    Alcide Bava
    A. R.

JULY 14, 1871

Le bateau ivre

Comme je descendais des Fleuves impassibles,
Je ne me sentis plus guidé par les haleurs:
Des Peaux-Rouges criards les avaient pris pour cibles
Les ayant cloués nus aux poteaux de couleurs.

J'étais insoucieux de tous les équipages,
Porteur de blés flamands ou de cotons anglais
Quand avec mes haleurs ont fini ces tapages
Les Fleuves m'ont laissé descendre où je voulais.

Dans les clapotements furieux des marées
Moi, l'autre hiver plus sourd que les cerveaux d'enfants
Je courus! Et les Péninsules démarrées
N'ont pas subi tohu-bohus plus triomphants

La tempête a béni mes éveils maritimes
Plus léger qu'un bouchon j'ai dansé sur les flots
Qu'on appelle rouleurs éternels de victimes,
Dix nuits, sans regretter l'œil niais des falots!

Plus douce qu'aux enfants la chair des pommes sures
L'eau verte pénétra ma coque de sapin
Et des taches de vins bleus et des vomissures
Me lava, dispersant gouvernail et grappin.

Et dès lors, je me suis baigné dans le Poème
De la Mer, infusé d'astres et lactescent,
Dévorant les azurs vers; où, flottaison blême
Et ravie, un noyé pensif parfois descend;

Où, teignant tout à coup les bleuités, délires
Et rythmes lents sous les rutilements du jour,
Plus fortes que l'alcool, plus vastes que nos lyres
Fermentent les rousseurs amères de l'amour!

The Drunken Boat

As I was flowing down impassive rivers, meek,
the lines from my haulers slackened! yelping Redskins
had butchered them, targets of a vile hide-and-seek,
hung them naked from colored poles, scalps shorn, dormant.

I cared nothing for crews, attendants, galley slaves,
nothing for Flemish wheat or my English linens;
when this business with my haulers ceased, the waves
furthered my descent—I, loosed in the River's bends!

Into the violent whips and wrack of crashing tides
I, the other Winter, an apoplectic child,
I ran! peninsulas unmoored from Pangaea's slides
had never witnessed such a tohu-bohu, wild.

In flowed benedictions for my maritime wiles.
Light as a dancing cork, I bobbed atop the crests,
those famed rollers of victims; for ten days exiled,
with no thought of the lighthouse's eye—that nonsense!

The water bathed my hull of fir, aglaeic, green,
was as sweet as sour fruit to children nursed on brine.
Wave froth seared me, cleansed me of vomit and blue wine,
flushed me, churning in whirlpools keel, rudder and line.

From that day on, I bathed only in the Poem
of the Sea, flush with stars vacating, lactescent,
absorbing the blue verse—where, like a bleached out stem,
mere flotsam, a pale corpse seeks its quiet descent.

Suddenly, where the blue is dyed by delirium
and morose rhythms streak under hymns of daylight,
grander than liquor, vaster than the kettle drum,
the scarlet pip of love illuminates the night.

Je sais les cieux crevant en éclairs, et les trombes
Et les ressacs et les courants: je sais le soir,
L'Aube exaltée ainsi qu'un peuple de colombes
Et j'ai vu quelquefois ce que l'homme a cru voir!

J'ai vu le soleil bas, taché d'horreurs mystiques,
Illuminant de longs figements violets,
Pareils à des acteurs de drames très-antiques
Les flots roulant au loin leurs frissons de volets!

J'ai rêvé la nuit verte aux neiges éblouies
Baiser montant aux yeux des mers avec lenteurs,
La circulation des sèves inouïes
Et l'éveil jaune et bleu des phosphores chanteurs!

J'ai suivi, des mois pleins, pareille aux vacheries
Hystériques, la houle à l'assaut des récifs,
Sans songer que les pieds lumineux des Maries
Pussent forcer le mufle aux Océans poussifs!

J'ai heurté, savez-vous, d'incroyables Florides
Mêlant aux fleurs des yeux de panthères à peaux
D'hommes! Des arcs-en-ciel tendus comme des brides
Sous l'horizon des mers, à de glauques troupeaux!

J'ai vu fermenter les marais énormes, nasses
Où pourrit dans les joncs tout un Léviathan!
Des écroulements d'eaux au milieu des bonaces,
Et les lointains vers les gouffres cataractant!

Glaciers, soleils d'argent, flots nacreux, cieux de braises!
Échouages hideux au fond des golfes bruns
Où les serpents géants dévorés des punaises
Choient, des arbres tordus, avec de noirs parfums!

J'aurais voulu montrer aux enfants ces dorades
Du flot bleu, ces poissons d'or, ces poissons chantants.

I know the skies regnant with claws of branched lightning,
eddies, spouts, and currents; I know crippled evening;
I know dawn exalted with dove's flight, aspiring,
I've seen what men thought they saw, self-preening.

I've seen the sun, gloaming over fogged horizons,
mystic, illuminated with violent figments
shuffling like a chorus with ancient overtones,
their plaints spiraling off into tragic fragments.

I've dreamed a green night with enrapturing snows,
a kiss rising slowly to the brow of the sea;
I've dreamed the movement of secret amber flows
and phosphorescent songs in a blue, yellow key.

During gnashed, pregnant months I followed waves rising
like hysterical cows assaulting coral reefs,
not dreaming the coy knees of those Marys reclining
could ward off the Ocean's patriarchal beliefs!

I charged, you know, against fathomless Floridas
amid flowers with panther's eyes, and clothed with skins
of men! and bridal trains of dilating rainbows
leading to emerald herds beneath the sun's horizons.

I have seen, reaching miles, swamps ferment, rank fish-traps,
—a whole Leviathan now a plucked, pink carcass!—
waters avalanching in a drape of cloud mist,
and distant Niagaras scraping a blank Abyss.

Glaciers, silver suns, milk-white waves, embers dying
in the skies! hideous toxic beaches, rank brown;
enormous snakes, gnawed at by bedbugs, descending
eucalyptus trees with a black, ignoble sound.

I'd thought, one day, to show children the sunfish
riding a blue wave, the golden fish, the singing fish!

—Des écumes de fleurs ont bercé mes dérades
Et d'ineffables vents m'ont ailé par instants.

Parfois, martyr lassé des pôles et des zones,
La mer dont le sanglot faisait mon roulis doux
Montait vers moi ses fleurs d'ombre aux ventouses jaunes
Et je restais, ainsi qu'une femme à genoux...

Presque île, ballottant sur mes bords les querelles
Et les fientes d'oiseaux clabaudeurs aux yeux blonds
Et je voguais, lorsqu'à travers mes liens frêles
Des noyés descendaient dormir, à reculons!

Or moi, bateau perdu sous les cheveux des anses,
Jeté par l'ouragan dans l'éther sans oiseau
Moi dont les Monitors et les voiliers des Hanses
N'auraient pas repêché la carcasse ivre d'eau;

Libre, fumant, monté de brumes violettes,
Moi qui trouais le ciel rougeoyant comme un mur,
Qui porte, confiture exquise aux bons poètes,
Des lichens de soleil et des morves d'azur,

Qui courais, taché de lunules électriques,
Planche folle, escorté des hippocampes noirs,
Quand les juillets faisaient crouler à coups de triques
Les cieux ultramarins aux ardents entonnoirs;

Moi qui tremblais, sentant geindre à cinquante lieues
Le rut des Béhémots et les Maelstroms épais,
Fileur éternel des immobilités bleues,
Je regrette l'Europe aux anciens parapets!

J'ai vu des archipels sidéraux! et des îles
Dont les cieux délirants sont ouverts au vogueur:
—Est-ce en ces nuits sans fond que tu dors et t'exiles,
Million d'oiseaux d'or ô future Vigueur?—

—Flowers of foam pitched me out of this sly wish;
ineffable winds winged me, idle thoughts to vanquish.

At times a martyr, I tired of poles and zones,
drugged by the tidal roll of the sobbing, gentle sea
that brought me dark blooms flecked with yellow stamens;
and so I rested, a peasant woman on her knees.

Like an island bearing on my cliffs the clamor
and guano of loud birds with yellow, feral eyes;
and on I sailed when the distinct, sickly pallor
of drowned men flicked my ropes, then sank, unparalyzed.

So I, perishing in the lianas of sea caves
or flung into birdless air by stinging monsoon,
I, who no Customs, no Hanseatic clipper saves,
whose water-drunk carcass teeters, an errant moon.

Free, but smoldering, topped with a violet cloud,
I, who stormed reddened skies like castle walls,
I, who bore sweet manna for the attentive poet,
lichens culled from sunlight! phlegm from true indigos!

Who ran, piebalded with tiny electric orbs,
an unleashed plank, borne on the seahorse's ribbed sides,
when Julys descended with cudgel blows, and storms
rose with fiery funnels to ultramarine skies.

I who, trembling, heard through expanses of fifty leagues
the moan of the Cyclops in heat, the Maelstroms' jests,
endless filimenter of blue immobility,
fool! now sick for Europe, its stony parapets.

Archipelagos like clusters of swimming stars
whose skies buzz with deliria of voyagers,
is it in this depthless well, you, oh golden birds
sleep out your exile, oh you future shining Vigor?

Mais, vrai, j'ai trop pleuré! Les Aubes sont navrantes
Toute lune est atroce et tout soleil amer:
L'âcre amour m'a gonflé de torpeurs enivrantes
Ô que ma quille éclate! ô que j'aille à la mer!

Si je désire une eau d'Europe, c'est la flache
Noire et froide où vers le crépuscule embaumé
Un enfant accroupi plein de tristesses, lâche
Un bateau frêle comme un papillon de mai.

Je ne puis plus, baigné de vos langueurs, ô lames,
Enlever leur sillage aux porteurs de cotons,
Ni traverser l'orgueil des drapeaux et des flammes,
Ni nager sous les yeux horribles des pontons.

It's true: I cry too much. Each dawn brings me to tears,
each moon is atrocious, each sun, sour misery;
acrid love distills me with enervating fears;
oh, that the floorboards burst! that I'm rent by the sea!

If there is a water of Europe that I crave
it is a black puddle, cold, in sweet-smelling night
where a sad child, squatting, sets forth on its way
a folded boat, fragile as a May butterfly.

Never again can I, oh waves, embalmed in sleep,
ride fast into the wakes of English cotton boats
nor cross nations' borders, their torches, flags, and keeps
nor swim by prison hulks that taunt me with their ropes.

SUMMER, 1871

Oraison du soir

Je vis assis, tel qu'un ange aux mains d'un barbier,
Empoignant une chope à fortes cannelures,
L'hypogastre et le col cambrés, une Gambier
Aux dents, sous l'air gonflé d'impalpables voilures.

Tels que les excréments chauds d'un vieux colombier,
Mille Rêves en moi font de douces brûlures:
Puis par instants mon cœur triste est comme un aubier
Qu'ensanglante l'or jeune et sombre des coulures.

Puis, quand j'ai ravalé mes rêves avec soin,
Je me tourne, ayant bu trente ou quarante chopes,
Et me recueille, pour lâcher l'âcre besoin:

Doux comme le Seigneur du cèdre et des hysopes,
Je pisse vers les cieux bruns très haut et très loin,
Avec l'assentiment des grands héliotropes.

Evening Prayer

Seated, I thrive—cherubic, as if in the grip
of a barber, fist curled around a fluted mug,
my neck and hypogastrium arched, Gambier pipe
in my jaw—the air thick with impalpable smoke!

Like the fresh droppings in a rickety birdhouse,
a Thousand Dreams coddle me, warm with their promise.
Often, the spirit courses like virgin sapwood
bloodied by the young, cloudy gold of its seepage.

Then, when I have imbibed—impeccably—my dreams,
having downed thirty or forty mugs, I come to
and collect myself—to relieve the bitter need!

Courtly, a high Lord of the cedar and hyssop,
I piss toward somber skies, very lofty, far off,
that sun-whore bloom approving—the heliotrope!

1870-1872

Les mains de Jeanne-Marie

Jeanne-Marie a des mains fortes,
Mains sombres que l'été tanna,
Mains pâles comme des mains mortes.
—Sont-ce des mains de Juana?

Ont-elles pris les crèmes brunes
Sur les mares des voluptés?
Ont-elles trempé dans des lunes
Aux étangs de sérénités?

Ont-elles bu des cieux barbares,
Calmes sur les genoux charmants?
Ont-elles roulé des cigares
Ou trafiqué des diamants?

Sur les pieds ardents des Madones
Ont-elles fané des fleurs d'or?
C'est le sang noir des belladones
Qui dans leur paume éclate et dort.

Mains chasseresses des diptères
Dont bombinent les bleuisons
Aurorales, vers les nectaires?
Mains décanteuses de poisons?

Oh! quel Rêve les a saisies
Dans les pandiculations?
Un rêve inouï des Asies,
Des Khenghavars ou des Sions?

—Ces mains n'ont pas vendu d'oranges,
Ni bruni sur les pieds des dieux:
Ces mains n'ont pas lavé les langes
Des lourds petits enfants sans yeux.

The Hands of Jeanne-Marie

Jeanne-Marie has strong dark hands,
hands olived by the summer.
Colorless hands like dead hands.
Are they the hands of Donna Juana?

A chocolate-cream brown, did they
sail on ponds of carnal pleasure?
Did they dive after the moons
shimmering in lakes of leisure?

Have they drunk in barbarous skies,
calm, upon enchanting knees?
Have they rolled giant cigars,
or trafficked in diamond deals?

Have they, at the feet of Madonnas
tossed stems of golden flowers?
The black blood of belladonnas
explodes, then sleeps in their palms.

Are they the hands that drive the diptera
that buzzes the dawn's blueness,
direct them toward the nectar?
Are they hands that uncork poisons?

Oh, what Dream has consumed them
with wide pandiculations?
Some savage dream of the Asias,
or of Khenghavars, or Zions?

These hands have not sold oranges
or bronzed at the feet of gods,
these hands have washed no rag stained
by chubby, eyeless toddlers!

(Ce ne sont pas mains de cousine
Ni d'ouvrières aux gros fronts
Que brûle, aux bois puant l'usine,
Un soleil ivre de goudrons)

Ce sont des ployeuses d'échines,
Des mains qui ne font jamais mal
Plus fatales que des machines,
Plus fortes que tout un cheval!

Remuant comme des fournaises,
Et secouant tous ses frissons
Leur chair chante des Marseillaises
Et jamais les Eleisons!

(Ça serrerait vos cous, ô femmes
Mauvaises, ça broierait vos mains
Femmes nobles, vos mains infâmes
Pleines de blancs et de carmins

L'éclat de ces mains amoureuses
Tourne le crâne des brebis!
Dans leurs phalanges savoureuses
Le grand soleil met un rubis!)

Une tache de populace
Les brunit comme un sein d'hier;
Le dos de ces Mains est la place
Qu'en baisa tout Révolté fier!

Elles ont pâli, merveilleuses,
Au grand soleil d'amour chargé,
Sur le bronze des mitrailleuses
À travers Paris insurgé!

Ah! quelquefois, ô Mains sacrées,
À vos poings, Mains où tremblent nos

These are not a courtesan's hands,
nor of toiling women, skins peeled
by a star wasted on tar smells
in factory-stinking woods.

These are the slanters of backbones,
hands that can never do harm
—more absolute than the machine,
more powerful than the horse!

Whistling like furnaces,
shaking off terror spasms,
their flesh sings Marseillaises,
and not Kyrie Eleisons!

They could snap your necks, oh evil
women! pulverize your hands,
countesses! your hands renowned
for shades of white and carmine.

The splendor of these loving hands
swivels the heads of the ewes!
On their savory phalanxes
the great sun installs a ruby!

The blemish of the hoi polloi
browns them like the breasts of yore;
to kiss this flesh is the joy
every proud Rebel desires!

These hands have paled, so stunning
in the sun charged with the cause,
on the bronze skins of machine-guns
throughout insurgent Paris!

Ah, sometimes, oh sacred Hands,
at your wrists where dances our

Lèvres jamais désenivrées,
Crie une chaîne aux clairs anneaux!

Et c'est un soubresaut étrange
Dans nos êtres, quand, quelquefois,
On veut vous déhâler, Mains d'ange,
En vous faisant saigner les doigts!

Fév. 72

lips that are never sober
a chain of bright rings cries out!

There is a strange Convulsion
in our beings when, at times,
they want to bleach your tans, Hands
of angels—by bleeding your thumbs!

FEBRUARY, 1872

"L'étoile a pleuré…"

L'étoile a pleuré rose au cœur de tes oreilles,
L'infini roulé blanc de ta nuque à tes reins
La mer a perlé rousse à tes mammes vermeilles
Et l'Homme saigné noir à ton flanc souverain.

"The star wept..."

The star wept, roseate, into the heart of your ears,
white Infinity streamed from your lips to your loins,
the sea bubbled red astride your crimson nipples,
and Man hemorrhaged black upon your sovereign hips.

1870-1872

6: POEMS FROM

THE "ALBUM ZUTIQUE"

Thanks for your letter, and hosannas for your "prayer." OF COURSE, we'll see each other again! When?—Wait a bit! Hard necessity! Stern circumstances! That's all right! And shit on some, shit on others! And like shit on me! And on you!

—Paul Verlaine to Rimbaud, April 1872

L'Idole. Sonnet du trou du cul

Obscur et froncé comme un œillet violet
Il respire, humblement tapi parmi la mousse.
Humide encor d'amour qui suit la fuite douce
Des Fesses blanches jusqu'au cœur de son ourlet.

Des filaments pareils à des larmes de lait
Ont pleuré, sous le vent cruel qui les repousse,
À travers de petits caillots de marne rousse
Pour s'aller perdre où la pente les appelait.

Mon Rêve s'aboucha souvent à sa ventouse;
Mon âme, du coït matériel jalouse,
En fit son larmier fauve et son nid de sanglots.

C'est l'olive pâmée, et la flûte câline;
C'est le tube où descend la céleste praline:
Chanaan féminin dans les moiteurs enclos!

    Albert Mérat
    P. V. - A. R.

Idol. Sonnet to the Asshole

In dark shadows, wrinkled, like a crevassed violet,
it breathes contentedly, silly among the reeds,
still moist with the love it most recently received,
white buttocks coursing from their inclines to its edge.

Filaments straggle like hot wet weepings of milk
which the cruel wind banishes to a life of flight
over small plots of marl that, reddish, in their height,
confuse and distract them—they fall like battered silk.

In my dreams, my mouth was poised above its abyss;
my soul, envious of physical coitus,
usurped it for sobs—a bottle for tear-tincture.

An aromatic olive—or seductive flute—
chute down which currents of heavenly praline shoot—
a feminine Canaan—bedewed by sharp moisture!

    Albert Mérat
    P. V. - A. R.

Lys

O balancoirs! o lys! clysopompes d'argent!
Dédaigneux des travaux, dédaigneux des famines!
L'Aurore vous emplit d'un amour détergent!
Une douceur de ciel beurre vos étamines!

Armand Silvestre
A.R.

Lily

Oh seesaws! Oh lily! Silver enema pumps!
Disdainful of all work! Disdainful of famines!
Morning fills you with its disinfectant love!
A sweetness from heaven butters your stamens!

Armand Silvestre
A.R.

Vu à Rome

Il est, à Rome, à la Sixtine,
Couverte d'emblèmes chrétiens,
Une cassette écarlatine
Où sèchent des nez fort anciens:

Nez d'ascètes de Thébaïde,
Nez de chanoines du Saint Graal
Où se figea la nuit livide,
Et l'ancien plain-chant sépulcral.

Dans leur sécheresse mystique,
Tous les matins, on introduit
De l'immondice schismatique
Qu'en poudre fine on a réduit.

    Leon Dierx
    A. R.

Seen in Rome

In the Sistine in Rome, there sits,
covered in Christian emblems,
a scarlet casket where ancient
noses lie and dehydrate:

noses of Thebaid ascetics,
noses of the canons of
the Holy Grail... the white nights thick
with old, sepulchral plain-chants.

Into their mystic aridness
is poured every morning
a schismatic rubbish that has
been ground into a fine powder.

    Leon Dierx
    A. R.

Fête galante

Rêveur, Scapin
Gratte un lapin
Sous sa capote.

Colombina,
—Que l'on pina!—
—Do, mi, —tapote

L'œil du lapin
Qui tôt, tapin,
Est en ribote...

    Paul Verlaine
    A. R.

Love Feast

Dreaming, Scapin
shakes a rabbit
beneath his cape.

Colombina
—who just got laid!—
Do, mi—taps on

the rabbit's eye
which, like a drum,
gets very tight...

      Paul Verlaine
      A. R.

"J'occupais un wagon de troisième…"

J'occupais un wagon de troisième: un vieux prêtre
Sortit son brûle-gueule et mit à la fenêtre,
Vers les brises, son front très calme aux poils pâlis.
Puis ce chrétien, bravant les brocarts impolis,
S'étant tourné, me fit la demande énergique
Et triste en même temps d'une petite chique
De caporal, —ayant été l'aumônier chef
D'un rejeton royal condamné derechef;—
Pour malaxer l'ennui d'un tunnel, sombre veine
Qui s'offre aux voyageurs, près Soissons, ville d'Aisne.

"I occupied a third class car..."

I occupied a third class car when an old priest
took out his pipe. He bent his calm brow and meager
hair outside the window, into the breeze. And then
this Christian, unaware of the others' unease,
turned to face me and, sadly, yet intimately,
asked if I might spare some tobacco, just a pinch
—he once having been, he related, the chaplain
of a man twice-condemned, a famed royal scion—
to ease the boredom of this tunnel, a dark vein
mined for travelers near Soissons, town of the Aisne.

"Je préfère sans doute..."

Je préfère sans doute, au printemps, la guinguette
Où des marronniers nains bourgeonne la baguette,
Vers la prairie étroite et communale, au mois
De mai. Des jeunes chiens rabroués bien des fois
Viennent près des Buveurs triturer des jacinthes
De plate-bande. Et c'est, jusqu'aux soirs d'hyacinthe,
Sur la table d'ardoise où, l'an dix-sept cent vingt
Un diacre grava son sobriquet latin
Maigre comme une prose à des vitraux d'église
La toux des flacons noirs qui jamais ne les grise.

François Copée
A. R.

"Without doubt I prefer..."

Without doubt I prefer, in spring, outdoor cafes
where dwarf chestnut trees start to offer up their leaves
in the narrow meadows that common people share
in May. Young dogs, scolded often, yet who don't care,
scramble near the Drinkers, trample the hyacinths
in their beds. There stands, in the hyacinthine dark,
on the slate table—where, in seventeen-twenty,
a deacon engraved his Latin nickname, slight as
the lines one sees inscribed on the panes of churches—
the coughing of black flasks that never make them drunk.

François Copée
A. R.

"L'Humanité chaussait ..."

L'Humanité chaussait le vaste enfant Progrès.

Louis-Xavier de Ricard
A. Rimbaud

"Humanity put shoes..."

Humanity put shoes on the huge child Progress.

Louis-Xavier de Ricard
A. Rimbaud

Conneries

1. Jeune goinfre

Casquette
De moire,
Quéquette
D'ivoire,

Toilette
Très noire,
Paul guette
L'armoire,

Projette
Languette
Sur poire,

S'apprête
Baguette,
Et foire

    A. R.

Crude Jokes

1. YOUNG GLUTTON

Silken
beret,
penis
ivory,

ink black
couture,
Paul guards
cupboards,

projects
his tongue
at pears,

prepares
his stick,
then dungs!

    A. R.

2. Paris

Al. Godillot, Gambier,
Galopeau, Volf-Pleyel,
—Ô Robinets! —Menier,
—Ô Christs! —Leperdriel!

Kinck, Jacob, Bonbonnel!
Veuillot, Tropmann, Augier!
Gill, Mendès, Manuel,
Guido Gonin! —Panier

Des Grâces! L'Hérissé!
Cirages onctueux!
Pains vieux, spiritueux!

Aveugles! —puis, qui sait?—
Sergents de ville, Enghiens
Chez soi! —soyons chrétiens!

    A. R.

2. Los Angeles

H&M, Wolfgang Puck,
Payless Shoes, Sephora,
—Oh Ralphs!—Banana Republic!
—Oh Christs! Ikea!

Cat Eye, Manson, Costco!
Tate, Gamestop, Ed
Ruscha! Pinches—Jumbo's!
—Vangelisti! —Basket

of the graces! IMAX!
Oh, unctuous waxes!
Old bread loaves, spirits!

The blind!—But who can say?—
Cops, La Poubelle—Cugurt
Door Dashed! —Let's be Christians!

    B.K.S.
    For Román Luján

Conneries 2e Série

1. Cocher ivre

Pouacre
Boit:
Nacre
Voit:

Âcre
Loi,
Fiacre
Choit!

Femme
Tombe:
Lombe

Saigne:
—Clame!
Geigne.

A. R.

Crude Jokes, 2nd Series

1. THE DRUNKEN COACHMAN

Creeps
drink:
pearls
blink:

strict
law,
wheels
jolt!

Girl
falls,
loins

bleed:
—Howl!
Groan.

    A. R.

Vieux de la vieille!

Aux paysans de l'empereur!
À l'empereur des paysans!
    Au fils de Mars,
    Au glorieux 18 *Mars*!
Où le Ciel d'Eugénie a béni les entrailles!

The Old Man of the Old Woman!

To the emperor's peasants!
To the emperor of the peasants!
   To the sons of Mars,
     to the glorious 18th of *March*!
when Heaven blessed the entrails of Eugenie!

État de siège?

Le pauvre postillon, sous le dais de fer-blanc,
Chauffant une engelure énorme sous son gant,
Suit son lourd omnibus parmi la rive gauche,
Et de son aine en flamme écarte la sacoche.
Et tandis que, douce ombre où des gendarmes sont,
L'honnête intérieur regarde au ciel profond
La lune se bercer parmi la verte ouate,
Malgré l'édit et l'heure encore délicate,
Et que l'omnibus rentre à l'Odéon, impur
Le débauché glapit au carrefour obscur!

François Copée
A. R.

State of Siege?

The poor postilion beneath a tin cover
warms a huge chilblain in his glove. He ushers
his heavy omnibus beside the left bank
and keeps his money purse from irritating
his engorged groin. Police loom in soft shadows.
Honest folks inside gaze up into the deep
sky where the moon is cradled in woolly green.
And despite the curfew, the delicate hour,
the bus just returning to the Odeon,
an enraged pervert screams in the darkened square.

François Copée
A. R.

Le balai

C'est un humble balai de chiendent, trop dur
Pour une chambre ou pour la peinture d'un mur.
L'usage en est navrant et ne vaut pas qu'on rie.
Racine prise à quelque ancienne prairie
Son crin inerte sèche: et son manche a blanchi.
Tel un bois d'île à la canicule rougi.
La cordelette semble une tresse gelée.
J'aime de cet objet la saveur désolée
Et j'en voudrais laver tes larges bords de lait,
O Lune où l'esprit de nos Sœurs mortes se plaît.

    F. C.

The Brush

It is a humble scrub brush, too unrefined
for a dresser, or to kiss a wall with paint.
Its uses? Ugh, awful! But we should not laugh.
Its bristles dried out, stiff, as if it were scruff
from some ancient field. Its handle has grown pale.
Like an island wood reddened by a heat wave;
a little cord that looks like a frozen braid.
I love this object's desolate air—I'd love
to use it to wash your large milk sides, oh moon,
where the souls of our dead Sisters like to stay!

    F. C.

Exil

. . . .

Que l'on s'intéressa souvent, mon cher Conneau!...
Plus qu'à l'Oncle Vainqueur, au Petit Ramponneau!...
Que tout honnête instinct sort du Peuple débile!...
Hélas!! Et qui a fait tourner mal notre bile!...
Et qu'il nous sied déjà de pousser le verrou
Au Vent que les enfants nomment Bari-barou!...

. . . .

Fragment d'une épître en Vers de Napoléon III, 1871

Exile

. . . .

That one was often interested, dear Conneau!...
More than in Uncle Rout, in little Ramponneau!...
That the best instincts arise from the low people!...
Alas! Those who made our stomachs nervous with bile!...
And now, we should lock our doors with an iron bolt
against that wind the children call Bari-Barou!...

. . . .

Fragment of an epistle in Verse by Napoleon III, 1871

.

L'angelot maudit

Toits bleuâtres et portes blanches
Comme en de nocturnes dimanches,

Au bout de la ville sans bruit,
La Rue est blanche, et c'est la nuit.

La Rue a des maisons étranges
Avec des persiennes d'Anges.

Mais, vers une borne, voici
Accourir, mauvais et transi,

Un noir Angelot qui titube,
Ayant trop mangé de jujube.

Il fait caca: puis disparaît:
Mais son caca maudit paraît,

Sous la lune sainte qui vaque,
De sang sale un léger cloaque!

    Louis Ratisbonne
    A. Rimbaud

The Cursed Cherub

Near the town's edge, the roofs are blue,
doors white, as on a typical

Sunday evening. It is quiet.
The street is white, and it is night.

The homes that line the street are odd,
—as if angels barred the windows.

But look! There runs toward a fence post,
blubbering and full of malice,

a dark cherub who dips and weaves—
he's had too many jujubes!

He takes a dump, then disappears,
leaving behind a pile that gleams

in the moonlight, vacant, holy,
—a small cesspool of befouled blood.

        Louis Ratisbonne
        A. Rimbaud

"Les soirs d'été..."

Les soirs d'été, sous l'œil ardent des devantures
Quand la sève frémit sous les grilles obscures
Irradiant au pied des grêles marronniers,
Hors de ces groupes noirs, joyeux ou casaniers,
Suceurs du brûle-gueule ou baiseurs du cigare,
Dans le kiosque mi-pierre étroit où je m'égare,
—Tandis qu'en haut rougoie une annonce d'*Ibled*,—
Je songe que l'hiver figera le Filet
D'eau propre qui bruit, apaisant l'onde humaine,
—Et que l'âpre aquilon n'épargne aucune veine.

    François Copée
    A. Rimbaud

"Summer nights..."

Summer nights, under the burning eye of storefronts,
when the sap simmers beneath the warren of roots
radiating at the base of thin chestnut trees—
near those dark groves, joyous men or stay-at-home dads,
some suckers of short pipes, some kissers of cigars,
in the tight, semi-stone kiosk where I wander—
above, an *Ibled* advertisement flashes red—
I think that winter will freeze the small Rivulet
of clear water that flows, pleasing the human wave,
and that the harsh north wind will not spare any vein.

François Copée
A. Rimbaud

"Aux livres de chevet..."

Aux livres de chevet, livres de l'art serein,
Obermann et Genlis, Vert-Vert et le Lutrin,
Blasé de nouveauté grisâtre et saugrenue,
J'espère, la vieillesse étant enfin venue,
Ajouter le traité du Docteur Venetti.
Je saurai, revenu du public abêti,
Goûter le charme ancien des dessins nécessaires.
Ecrivain et graveur ont doré les misères
Sexuelles, et c'est, n'est-ce pas, cordial:
Dr VENETTI, *Traité de l'Amour conjugal.*

F. Copée
A. R.

"To My Bedside Collection..."

To my bedside collection, my books of fine art,
Obermann and Genlis, the *Lutrin* and *Ver-Vert*,
and bored with strange novelties that no longer please,
I hope, now in my golden age, to finally
add them the Oeuvre by Dr. Venetti.
Withdrawn from the thick-witted public, I will be
able to absorb the fine drawings like a fuel.
Author and engraver have distilled the sexual
miseries, and that's what most buoys the soul up:
—Dr. VENETTI: *Treatise on Conjugal Love.*

F. Copée
A. R.

Hypotyposes saturniennes,
ex Belmontet

———————

Quel est donc ce mystère impénétrable et sombre?
Pourquoi, sans projeter leur voile blanche, sombre
    Tout jeune esquif royal gréé?

———————

Renversons la douleur de nos lacrymatoires. ———————

. . . .

——————— L'amour veut vivre aux dépens de sa sœur,
    L'amitié vit aux dépens de son frère.

. . . .

Le sceptre, qu'à peine on révère, ———————
N'est que la croix d'un grand calvaire
Sur le volcan des nations!

———————

. . . .

Oh! l'honneur ruisselait sur ta mâle moustache. Belmontet,

    ——   archétype Parnassien.

Saturnian Hypotyposes,

From Belmontet

––––––––––

So, what is this inscrutable, somber mystery,
why does every rigged out royal skiff sink
   without putting out its jib?

––––––––––

Let's smash to the ground the pain of the lacrymatoires. ––––––––––

. . . .

––––––––– Love wants life at the expense of the sister.
    Friendship lives at the expense of the brother.

. . . .

The sceptre, that no one cares to praise, ––––––––––
is but a Calvary cross
on the volcano of nations!

––––––––––

. . . .

Oh, honor dripped like sweat down your manly mustache. Belmontet,

––––––––––   Parnassian archetype.

Les remembrances du vieillard idiot

Pardon, mon père!

          Jeune, aux foires de campagne,
Je cherchais, non le tir banal où tout coup gagne,
Mais l'endroit plein de cris où les ân[es, le flan]c
Fatigué, déployaient ce long tu[be] sa[ng]lant
Que je ne comprends pas encore!...

              [Et puis] ma mère,
Dont la chemise avait une sente[ur amè]re
Quoique fripée au bas et jaune co[mme u]n fruit,
Ma mère qui montait au lit avec [un] bruit
—Fils du travail pourtant, —ma mè[re, a]vec sa cuisse
De femme mûre, avec ses reins très [g]ros où plisse
Le linge, me donna ces chaleurs q[ue] l'on tait!...

Une honte plus crue et plus calme, c'était
Quand ma petite sœur, au retour de la classe,
Ayant usé longtemps ses sabots sur la glace,
Pissait, et regardait s'échapper de sa lèvre
D'en bas serrée et rose, un fil d'urine miève!...

O pardon!

        Je songeais à mon père parfois:
Le soir, le jeu de carte et les mots plus grivois,
Le voisin, et moi qu'on écartait, choses vues...
—Car un père est troublant! —et les choses conçues!..
Son genou, câlineur parfois; son pantalon
Dont mon doigt désirait ouvrir la fente,... —oh! non!—
Pour avoir le bout, gros, noir et dur, de mon père,
Dont la pileuse main me berçait!...

               Je veux taire
Le pot, l'assiette à manche, entrevue au grenier,
Les almanachs couverts en rouge, et le panier
De charpie, et la Bible, et les lieux, et la bonne,
La Sainte-Vierge et le crucifix...

Memories of an Old Moron

Oh forgive me, Father!
                When young, at country fairs,
I didn't loiter near games in which each dunk snares
a stuffed blue such-and-such, but near riotous stalls
where, exhausted, a donkey let his blood-tube sprawl
with wild brays—and I still don't know why!
                           And mother,
wearing an old chemise that bore a ripe odor,
frazzled at the bottom and yellow like a fruit,
my mother who leapt into bed with a loud hrumph!
—a genuine peasant!—my mother, with the thighs
of a proud country woman, whose fattened cheeks writhed
in the sheets—impressed me in ways wholly taboo!

But a calmer, yet cruder, shame was after school
when my little sister, back from her hide-and-seeks,
in boot heels shredded by the diamond winter ice,
pissed—and thrilled, as she watched the hot stream of urine
escape, steaming, from the pink lips beneath her spine...

Forgive me!
            —Naturally, I thought of my father,
at his card games, most nights barking obscene guffaws,
—my best friend—and myself!—they pushed off—but I saw...
—for a father is dark!—and the things one can know!—
his knees at times coaxing me, his trousers a draw,
and his fly my fingers wanted to pounce!—oh no!—
to have the thick hard cock of my swarthy father
whose hairy arms rocked me like a boat!
                         I will spare
you all the details—the Dutch oven, almanacs
with red covers, tins of lint, Bibles, the attics
I have known, long abandoned toilets, tiles, the maid,
the Virgin Mary and the Cross...

                          Oh! personne
Ne fut si fréquemment troublé, comme étonné!
Et maintenant, que le pardon me soit donné:
Puisque les sens infects m'ont mis de leurs victimes,
Je me confesse de l'aveu des jeunes crimes!...

· ·

Puis! —qu'il me soit permis de parler au Seigneur!
Pourquoi la puberté tardive et le malheur
Du gland tenace et trop consulté? Pourquoi l'ombre
Si lente au bas du ventre? et ces terreurs sans nombre
Comblant toujours la joie ainsi qu'un gravier noir?
—Moi j'ai toujours été stupéfait! Quoi savoir?

· ·

Pardonné?...
          Reprenez la chancelière bleue,
Mon père.
          O cette enfance! · · · · · · · · · · · · · ·
· ·
· —et tirons nous la queue!

    François Copée
    A. R.

                                    No one was hard
as often as I was, at least hourly slack-jawed!
And now, may Charity on me be full bestowed,
as my corrupt senses have branded me victim
—I confess—confess!—with tears—my juvenile crimes!
. . . .

Please, permit me to speak directly to the Lord!—
Why did puberty arrive so late, and why are
my coursing glands so often obeyed? Why the dark
that grows at the base of my gut? Why the terrors
burying my joys like black gravel? Even now,
I find ways to be shocked—is there more I should know?
. . . .

Forgiven?
              Here—take them—are your blue fleece foot muffs,
dear Father.
              What a childhood!. . . . .
. . . .
. . . . .Now let's go jerk off!

    François Copée
    A. R.

Ressouvenir

Cette année où naquit le Prince impérial
Me laisse un souvenir largement cordial
D'un Paris limpide où des N d'or et de neige
Aux grilles du palais, aux gradins du manège
Éclatent, tricolorement enrubannés.
Dans le remous public des grands chapeaux fanés,
Des chauds gilets à fleurs, des vieilles redingotes,
Et des chants d'ouvriers anciens dans les gargotes,
Sur des châles jonchés l'Empereur marche, noir
Et propre, avec la Sainte espagnole, le soir.

    François Copée

Remembrance

That year when the imperial Prince was born
leaves me with a memory I still adore:
of a clear Paris where N's of gold, with snow
at the palace gates, on the riding school's mounts,
burst forth with ribbons dyed with the tricolor.
In the public bustling of big faded hats,
warm vests embroidered with flowers, old frock coats
and songs of old workmen in all the dive bars,
the Emperor—proud, black—steps upon tossed shawls
with the Holy Spanish Woman in the night.

    François Copée

"L'Enfant qui ramassa les balles..."

L'Enfant qui ramassa les balles, le Pubère
Où circule le sang de l'exil et d'un Père
Illustre, entend germer sa vie avec l'espoir
De sa figure et de sa stature et veut voir
Des rideaux autres que ceux du Trône et des Crèches.
Aussi son buste exquis n'aspire pas aux brèches
De l'Avenir! —Il a laissé l'ancien jouet.
O son doux rêve ô son bel Enghien *! Son œil est
Approfondi par quelque immense solitude;
"Pauvre jeune homme, il a sans doute l'Habitude!"

      * parce que "Enghien chez soi"!

François Copée
†

"The child who picked up bullets..."

The child who picked up bullets, the Pubescent
in whom flows the blood of exile, his papa
quite famous, hears himself spoken of with hope
in his face and figure, and he wants to drape
curtains different than those at the Throne and Cribs.
His handsome head does not aspire to the brink
of the Future!—He has left the olden toy.
Oh, his sweet dream, oh, his fine Enghien*! His eye
is profound, darkened by some great solitude.
"Poor young man, doubtless he now has the Habit!"

* that is to say "Enghien for the home"!

François Copée
†

"Nos fesses ne sont pas les leurs..."

Nos fesses ne sont pas les leurs. Souvent j'ai vu
Des gens déboutonnés derrière quelque haie,
Et, dans ces bains sans gêne où l'enfance s'égaie,
J'observais le plan et l'effet de notre cul.

Plus ferme, blême en bien des cas, il est pouvu
De méplats évidents que tapisse la claie
Des poils; pour elles, c'est seulement dans la raie
Charmante que fleurit le long satin touffu.

Une ingéniosité touchante et merveilleuse
Comme l'on ne voit qu'aux anges des saints tableaux
Imite la joue où le sourire se creuse.

Oh! de même être nus, chercher joie et repos,
Le front tourné vers sa portion glorieuse,
Et libres tous les deux murmurer des sanglots?

"Our asses are not like theirs…"

Our asses are not like theirs! —One time, I would peer
behind a hedgerow to watch men with undone pants,
or watch, as they took their baths, carefree urchins dance,
and mark impressions of the gadget of the rear.

More firm, in many cases untanned, the shape
of the musculature is plain, though hid by tufts
of hair; for women, it is only in the cleft,
deep and charming, where such satin flowers erupt.

With an ingenious and disarming touch, as seen
in just the finest works of holy tapestry,
a dimple marks the cheek, as in a cherub's smile.

Oh, to be nude like that! to be drunk with the quest
for joy and rest! turned to a lover's missile test—
free in the dark murmurs of our sadness—a while!

1871-1872

"Les anciens animaux..."

Les anciens animaux saillissaient, même en course,
Avec des glands bardés de sang et d'excrément.
Nos pères étalaient leur membre fièrement
Par le pli de la gaine et le grain de la bourse.

Au moyen âge pour la femelle, ange ou pource,
Il fallait un gaillard de solide gréement;
Même un Kléber, d'après la culotte qui ment
Peut-être un peu, n'a pas dû manquer de ressource.

D'ailleurs l'homme au plus fier mammifère est égal;
L'énormité de leur membre à tort nous étonne;
Mais une heure stérile a sonné: le cheval

Et le bœuf ont bridé leurs ardeurs, et personne
N'osera plus dresser son orgueil génital
Dans les bosquets où grouille une enfance bouffonne.

"Animals, in ancient times..."

Animals, in ancient times, while on the go, fucked,
their hopping glands coated with blood and excrement.
Our forefathers paraded their cocks, content
the fold of the sheath, the weight of the package, talked.

In the Middle Ages, women—angels or sows—
sought a well-hung fellow; even Kléber was known
to wield a fine talon, a status overblown
in my mind, but perhaps he had employed voodoo.

Despite that, it's true: man competes with the mammal.
The hugeness of his dick is the wild beast's equal.
—Yet, a sterile hour has struck: the horse and the ox

have bridled genital lust, swamped with quietude.
There's no one left to dance, to frolic in the nude
with children in forests, gamboling amidst the phlox.

1871-1872

7: AFTER THE RAINS

I got used to elementary hallucination: I could very precisely see a mosque instead of a factory, a drum corps of angels, horse carts on the highways of the sky, a drawing room at the bottom of a lake; monsters and mysteries. A vaudeville's title filled me with awe.

—Rimbaud, "A Season in Hell"

Tête de faune

Dans la feuillée écrin vert taché d'or
Dans la feuillée incertaine et fleurie
De fleurs splendides où le baiser dort,
Vif et crevant l'exquise broderie,

Un faune effaré montre ses deux yeux
Et mord les fleurs rouges de ses dents blanches
Brunie et sanglante ainsi qu'un vin vieux
Sa lèvre éclate en rires sous les branches.

Et quand il a fui—tel qu'un écureuil—
Son rire tremble encore à chaque feuille
Et l'on voit épeuré par un bouvreuil
Le Baiser d'or du Bois, qui se recueille.

Faun's Head

In the foliage—a green spot flecked with gold—
in the uncertain foliage nurturing
delightful flowers... where a kiss drowses...
corrupting the sleepy setting—sprightly,

a terrified faun darts with two bright eyes
and bites the red flowers with strong, white teeth
bloodied and blemished, like from an old wine,
—his lips chortle beneath the canopy.

And when he's scampered off—like a squirrel—
his laughter still trembles on each green leaf.
You can see, unsettled by a bullfinch,
the Golden Kiss of the Woods urging peace.

1870-1872

Comedie de la soif

Nous sommes tes Grands-Parents,
    Les Grands!
Couverts des froides sueurs
De la lune et des verdures.
Nos vins secs avaient du cœur!
Au soleil sans imposture
Que faut-il à l'homme? boire.

Moi.—Mourir aux fleuves barbares.

Nous sommes tes Grands-Parents
    Des champs.
L'eau est au fond des osiers:
Vois le courant du fossé
Autour du Château mouillé.
Descendons en nos celliers;
Après, le cidre et le lait.

MOI.—Aller où boivent les vaches.

Nous sommes tes Grands-Parents;
    Tiens, prends
Les liqueurs dans nos armoires
Le Thé, le Café, si rares,
Frémissent dans les bouilloires.
—Vois les images, les fleurs.
Nous rentrons du cimetière.

MOI.—Ah! tarir toutes les urnes!

Comedy of Thirst

1. PARENTS

We are your Grandparents,
    the Grand!
dripping with the cold sweat
of the moon and greenery.
Our dry wines had heart!
In sunlight, completely frank,
what can a person do? Drink.

ME: Drown in barbarous rivers.

We are your Grandparents
    of pastures.
Water is deep in the osiers:
observe the fast moat-waters
that circle the moldy castle.
Let's descend to our cellars
—then later, milk and cider.

ME: Go where the cows slurp.

We are your Grandparents;
    come, enjoy
the liquors in our armoires.
The Tea, the Coffee, so rare,
simmer in our kettles.
—See the pictures, the flowers!
We're back from the cemetery.

ME: Ah! To lap dry the urns!

2. L'esprit

Éternelles Ondines
    Divisez l'eau fine.
Vénus, sœur de l'azur,
    Émeus le flot pur.

Juifs errants de Norwège
    Dites-moi la neige.
Anciens exilés chers
    Dites-moi la mer.

MOI.—Non, plus ces boissons pures,
    Ces fleurs d'eau pour verres.
Légendes ni figures
    Ne me désaltèrent;

Chansonnier, ta filleule
    C'est ma soif si folle
Hydre intime sans gueules
    Qui mine et désole.

2. MIND

Eternal ondines
    divide the clear water.
Venus, blue's sister,
    unsettles a pure wave.

Wandering Jews of Norway,
    tell me of the snow.
Tell me of the sea,
    dear ancient Outcasts.

ME: No, toss these pure quaffs,
    —water blooms for glasses!
No legends or icons
    can satisfy my thirst.

Singer, your goddaughter,
    is the thirst that burns,
candid, mouthless hydra
    that burrows and wastes.

3. Les Amis

Viens, les Vins vont aux plages,
Et les flots par millions!
Vois le Bitter sauvage
Rouler du haut des monts!
Gagnons, pèlerins sages,
L'absinthe aux verts piliers...

MOI.—Plus ces paysages.
Qu'est l'ivresse, Amis?

J'aime autant, mieux, même,
Pourrir dans l'étang,
Sous l'affreuse crème,
Près des bois flottants.

3. Friends

Come, on the shores flow Wines
with waves in the millions!
Behold, the wild Bitter
bounding down the mountains!
Take us, sage pilgrims,
to Absinthe's green pillars...

ME: Oh, ditch these panoramas!
What is drunkenness, sirs?

I'd as soon, even prefer,
to fester in a pond
rank with the fetid scum
by floating shards of wood.

4. Le Pauvre Songe

Peut-être un Soir m'attend
Où je boirai tranquille
En quelque vieille Ville,
Et mourrai plus content:
Puisque je suis patient!

Si mon mal se résigne,
Si j'ai jamais quelque or,
Choisirai-je le Nord
Ou le Pays des Vignes?...
—Ah! songer est indigne

Puisque c'est pure perte!
Et si je redeviens
Le voyageur ancien,
Jamais l'auberge verte
Ne peut bien m'être ouverte.

4. The Poor Dream

Perhaps a night awaits
when I shall drink in peace
in a lonely old town
and die more happily
because I am really patient!

If my sickness leaves me,
if I ever earn gold,
would I wander North, or
to the Land of Vineyards?
Ah! dreaming is such a canard

since it is purely loss!
And if, somehow revived,
I'm again a rover,
the green inn would never
reopen to me its old doors.

5. Conclusion

Les pigeons qui tremblent dans la prairie
Le gibier, qui court et qui voit la nuit,
Les bêtes des eaux, la bête asservie,
Les derniers papillons!... ont soif aussi

Mais fondre où fond ce nuage sans guide,
—Oh! favorisé de ce qui est frais!
Expirer en ces violettes humides
Dont les aurores chargent ces forêts?

Mai 1872

5. Conclusion

The pigeons fluttering in the pastures,
the game scrambling, peering through the dark,
the water animals, the beast enslaved,
the last butterflies—all have the same thirst!

Can't one just melt where the unguided cloud
melts, favored by the luxuriant cool,
then later expire in moistened violets
whose mornings infuse the waking forest?

MAY, 1872

Bonne pensée du matin

À quatre heures du matin, l'été,
Le sommeil d'amour dure encore.
Sous les bosquets l'aube évapore
    L'odeur du soir fêté.

Mais là-bas dans l'immense chantier
Vers le soleil des Hespérides,
En bras de chemise, les charpentiers
    Déjà s'agitent.

Dans leur désert de mousse, tranquilles,
Ils préparent les lambris précieux
Où la richesse de la ville
    Rira sous de faux cieux.

Ah! pour ces Ouvriers charmants
Sujets d'un roi de Babylone,
Vénus! laisse un peu les Amants.
    Dont l'âme est en couronne.

    Ô Reine des Bergers!
    Porte aux travailleurs l'eau-de-vie.
    Pour que leurs forces soient en paix
En attendant le bain dans la mer, à midi.

Mai 1872.

Good Thought in the Morning

At four o'clock on a summer morning,
the Sleep of love lingers over
the arbors, still; the dawn dissolves
    night's festive odors.

But below, at the building site beneath
a sun of the Hesperides,
carpenters in their shirtsleeves teem,
    already astir.

Within their desert of lichen, tranquil,
they prop up the costly panels.
The city's Esteemed will laugh there
    under false azures.

Ah! for these charming Laborers, subjects
of a Babylonian king,
Venus! leave your Lovers a sec,
    souls already ringed.

    Oh Queen of Shepherds!
    bring these Men their strong fruit liquors
    so that their strength find quietude
as they wait for the bath of the sea of noon!

MAY, 1872

La rivière de Cassis

La Rivière de Cassis roule ignorée
    En des vaux étranges:
La voix de cent corbeaux l'accompagne, vraie
    Et bonne voix d'anges:
Avec les grands mouvements des sapinaies
    Quand plusieurs vents plongent.

Tout roule avec des mystères révoltants
    De campagnes d'anciens temps:
De donjons visités, de parcs importants:
    C'est en ces bords qu'on entend
Les passions mortes des chevaliers errants:
    Mais que salubre est le vent!

Que le piéton regarde à ces claire-voies:
    Il ira plus courageux.
Soldats des forêts que le Seigneur envoie,
    Chers corbeaux délicieux!
Faites fuir d'ici le paysan matois
    Qui trinque d'un moignon vieux.

Mai 1872

The Cassis River

The Cassis River courses, unthought of,
  within strange valleys;
a hundred crows witness it, attentive,
  a pure angels' speech
in the great rustling of its fir groves
  when many winds breathe.

All flows within the heinous mysteries
  of ancient landscapes,
fortunes decided, legendary greens:
  on these banks, one hears
of failed passions, of knights in their folly
  —but the wind's so fair!

Let the walker peer through iron gates,
  go on more serene.
The forest's soldiers the Lord summons forth,
  dear, fawning ravens,
banish from here the offensive peasants
  who cheers! with stump-ends!

MAY, 1872

Larme

Loin des oiseaux, des troupeaux, des villageoises,
Je buvais, accroupi dans quelque bruyère
Entourée de tendres bois de noisetiers,
Par un brouillard d'après-midi tiède et vert.

Que pouvais-je boire dans cette jeune Oise,
Ormeaux sans voix, gazon sans fleurs, ciel couvert.
Que tirais-je à la gourde de colocase?
Quelque liqueur d'or, fade et qui fait suer

Tel, j'eusse été mauvaise enseigne d'auberge.
Puis l'orage changea le ciel, jusqu'au soir.
Ce furent des pays noirs, des lacs, des perches,
Des colonnades sous la nuit bleue, des gares.

L'eau des bois se perdait sur des sables vierges
Le vent, du ciel, jetait des glaçons aux mares...
Or! tel qu'un pêcheur d'or ou de coquillages,
Dire que je n'ai pas eu souci de boire!

Mai 1872

Tear

Far from the flocks, herds, and girls in the villages,
I drank, crouched down in a deep and scratchy heather,
encircled by the soft woods of the hazel tree;
that afternoon, I roamed in the fog, warm and green.

Oh, but what did I drink from that young river, Oise?
the mute elms, the flowerless grasses, the dark sky?
What quaff did I draw from the colocynth's ripe gourd?
A gold, insipid liquor—that made me perspire!

Yes, I would have made an ugly sign for an Inn!
Storms savaged the sky, grayed them out until evening.
Those were black countries—the lakes, the poles, the columns
of arches under the blue night, the train stations.

The water from the woods sank down into virgin sand.
The wind from the sky threw ice sheets over the lakes.
Yet! like a hunter for gold or for pretty shells,
don't say that I didn't care about my next drink!

MAY, 1872

Patience

D'UNE ÉTÉ.

Aux branches claires des tilleuls
Meurt un maladif hallali.
Mais des chansons spirituelles
Voltigent parmi les groseilles.
Que notre sang rie en nos veines
Voici s'enchevêtrer les vignes.
Le ciel est joli comme un ange
Azur et Onde communient.
Je sors! Si un rayon me blesse
Je succomberai sur la mousse.

Qu'on patiente et qu'on s'ennuie
C'est trop simple!... Fi de ces peines.
Je veux que l'été dramatique
Me lie à son char de fortune.
Que par toi beaucoup, O Nature,
—Ah moins nul et moins seul! je meure,
Au lieu que les bergers, c'est drôle,
Meurent à peu près par le monde.

Je veux bien que les saisons m'usent.
À Toi, Nature, je me rends,
Et ma faim et toute ma soif;
Et s'il te plaît, nourris, abreuve.
Rien de rien ne m'illusionne:
C'est rire aux parents qu'au soleil;
Mais moi je ne veux rire à rien
Et libre soit cette infortune.

Mai 1872

Patience

OF A SUMMER.

In the bright branches of lindens
the sickly hunting horn expires.
But a host of spirited songs
flutter among the currant shrubs.
Watch the vines grow entangled,
that our blood laugh in our veins!
The sky is pretty as an angel.
The azure and the wave commune.
I go out. And if I am wounded
by a sunbeam, I'll die on the moss.

Being patient and being bored
are too simple. Off with these cares!
I want a summer, dramatic,
to wield its chariot of fortune.
Due mostly to you, let me, oh Nature,
—ah, less alone and less useless!—die.
In shepherds' wolds, so odd,
they die all over the world.

I am fine if the seasons waste me.
To You, Nature, I surrender,
and my hunger and all my thirst
—if it so please, feed and water me.
Nothing fools me: to howl
at the sun is to howl at one's parents.
But I'm loathe to laugh at anything
—may this misfortune go free.

Chanson de la plus haute Tour

Oisive jeunesse
À tout asservie,
Par délicatesse
J'ai perdu ma vie.
Ah! Que le temps vienne
Où les cœurs s'éprennent.

Je me suis dit: laisse,
Et qu'on ne te voie:
Et sans la promesse
De plus hautes joies.
Que rien ne t'arrête
Auguste retraite.

J'ai tant fait patience
Qu'à jamais j'oublie;
Craintes et souffrances
Aux cieux sont parties.
Et la soif malsaine
Obscurcit mes veines.

Ainsi la Prairie
À l'oubli livrée,
Grandie, et fleurie
D'encens et d'ivraies
Au bourdon farouche
De cent sales mouches.

Ah! Mille veuvages
De la si pauvre âme
Qui n'a que l'image
De la Notre-Dame!
Est-ce que l'on prie
La Vierge Marie?

Idle youth, enslaved
to everything—by
being too sensitive
I have wasted my life.
Ah! Let the time come
when hearts fall in love!

I said to myself: let go,
let no one see you:
do without the hope
of any higher joys.
Let nothing delay your
august sanctuary.

I've been patient so long
I've forgotten all.
Fear and suffering
have fled to the clouds.
And an unhealthy need
now dims my veins.

Thus the meadow
given to oblivion,
full grown, flowering
with tares and incense,
to the wild buzzing
of a hundred filthy flies.

Oh! the thousand deaths
pressing the poor soul
that has only the image
of Our Lady!
Do people pray
to the Virgin Mary?

Oisive jeunesse
À tout asservie,
Par délicatesse
J'ai perdu ma vie.
Ah! Que le temps vienne
Où les cœurs s'éprennent!

Mai 1872

Idle youth, enslaved
to everything—by
being too sensitive
I have wasted my life.
Ah! Let the time come
when hearts fall in love!

L'ÉTERNITÉ

Elle est retrouvée.
Quoi?—L'Éternité.
C'est la mer allée
Avec le soleil.

Ame sentinelle,
Murmurons l'aveu
De la nuit si nulle
Et du jour en feu.

Des humains suffrages,
Des communs élans
Là tu te dégages
Et voles selon.

Puisque de vous seules,
Braises de satin,
Le Devoir s'exhale
Sans qu'on dise: enfin.

Là pas d'espérance,
Nul orietur
Science avec patience,
Le supplice est sûr.

Elle est retrouvée.
Quoi?—L'Éternité.
C'est la mer allée
Avec le soleil.

Mai 1872

ETERNITY

It has been found again.
What?—Eternity.
It is the sun
flown off with the sea.

Sentinel soul,
let us whisper the truth
about night full
of nothing—and day aflame.

Far from base urges,
from human approval,
you are free here
and run off as you will.

Since from you alone,
embers of satin,
Duty breathes without
anyone saying: at last.

Here, there is no hope,
no orietur.
Just science, patience.
—The suffering is sure.

It has been found again.
What?—Eternity.
It is the sun
flown off with the sea.

AGE D'OR

Quelqu'une des voix
Toujours angélique
—Il s'agit de moi,—
Vertement s'explique:

Ces mille questions
Qui se ramifient
N'amènent, au fond,
Qu'ivresse et folie;

Reconnais ce tour
Si gai, si facile:
Ce n'est qu'onde, flore,
Et c'est ta famille!

Puis elle chante. O
Si gai, si facile,
Et visible à l'œil nu...
—Je chante avec elle,—

Reconnais ce tour
Si gai, si facile,
Ce n'est qu'onde, flore,
Et c'est ta famille!... etc...

Et puis une voix
—Est-elle angélique!—
Il s'agit de moi,
Vertement s'explique;

Et chante à l'instant
En sœur des haleines:
D'un ton Allemand,
Mais ardente et pleine:

GOLDEN AGE

One of the voices
always angelic
—it's about myself—
strongly critiques:

those thousand questions
grown so rooted
just bring, in the end,
drunkenness and madness.

Understand this trick
so gay, so easy:
it is only a wave, a flower,
and that is your family!

Then it sings. Oh,
so gay, so easy,
and clearly visible...
—I join the chorus—

Understand this trick
so gay, so easy:
it is only a wave, a flower,
and that is your family!... etc...

One of the voices
—always angelic!—
goes on about myself,
strongly critiques,

and sings just now,
a sister to breath,
with Germanic tone,
but passionate and full:

Le monde est vicieux;
Si cela t'étonne!
Vis et laisse au feu
L'obscure infortune.

Ô! joli château!
Que ta vie est claire!
De quel Age es-tu
Nature princière
De Notre grand frère! etc....,

Je chante aussi, moi:
Multiples sœurs! Voix
Pas du tout publiques!
Environnez-moi
De gloire pudique... etc....,

Juin 1872

The world is vicious,
—if that surprises you
live and turn to ash
the obscene misfortune!

Oh! pretty castle!
How bright your life is!
From what Age hence?
Nature, so noble,
of Our elder brother! etc...

I also sing—me!
Diverse sisters! voices
entirely private
rain down upon me
with chaste glory... etc...

MAY-JUNE, 1872

Jeune ménage

La chambre est ouverte au ciel bleu-turquin;
Pas de place: des coffrets et des huches!
Dehors le mur est plein d'aristoloches
Où vibrent les gencives des lutins.

Que ce sont bien intrigues de génies
Cette dépense et ces désordres vains!
C'est la fée africaine qui fournit
La mûre, et les résilles dans les coins.

Plusieurs entrent, marraines mécontentes,
En pans de lumière dans les buffets,
Puis y restent! le ménage s'absente
Peu sérieusement, et rien ne se fait.

Le marié a le vent qui le floue
Pendant son absence, ici, tout le temps.
Même des esprits des eaux, malfaisants
Entrent vaguer aux sphères de l'alcôve.

La nuit, l'amie oh! la lune de miel
Cueillera leur sourire et remplira
De mille bandeaux de cuivre le ciel.
Puis ils auront affaire au malin rat

—S'il n'arrive pas un feu follet blême,
Comme un coup de fusil, après des vêpres.
—O spectres saints et blancs de Bethléem,
Charmez plutôt le bleu de leur fenêtre!

27 juin 1872

Young Couple

The room opens to the turquoise blue sky...
but there's no room! just boxes and hutches!
Birthwort ranges over the walls outside
where goblins gather and vibrate their gums.

This must be, one thinks, the ploys of genies,
this crazy expense, this wild disorder!
—Is it the African fairy who breeds
blackberries and hairnets in the corners?

Ill-humored godmothers in skirts of light
enter the cupboards in waves—where they stay!
The couple is out—interest is slight.
They're not serious. Much to do remains.

And the bridegroom has that wind that cheats him
when he's not in, like now—and all the time!
Water sprites, with a mischievous intent,
often fuss with the spheres of the bedroom.

At night—belovéd, oh!—the honeymoon
will gather up all their smiles and install
in the sky thousands of bright copper bands!
Then, they will have to face the crafty rat...

And if no pale will-o'-the-wisps can storm
like a cloud of grapeshot after vespers
—Oh holy white Spirits of Bethlehem,
promise to charm the blue of their windows!

JUNE 27, 1872

"Est-elle almée?..."

Est-Elle almée?... aux premières lueurs bleues
Se détruira-t-elle comme les fleurs feues...
Devant la splendide étendue où l'on sente
Souffler la ville énormément florissante!

C'est trop beau! c'est trop beau! mais c'est nécessaire
—Pour la Pêcheuse et la chanson du Corsaire,
Et aussi puisque les derniers masques crurent
Encore aux fêtes de nuit sur la mer pure!

Juillet 1872

"Is she an almeh?..."

Is she an almeh?—In the early blue hours,
will she snuff herself, like fire-flowers...
before the pageant of the city's aromas,
lavish and grand, the street's exhalations?

It's too much! Too beautiful! But we need it
—for the Sinful Woman, the Corsair's Song,
but also, since the last revelers believed,
even now, in soirées on the night's pure sea!

JULY, 1872

Fêtes de la faim

Ma faim, Anne, Anne,
Fuis sur ton âne.

Si j'ai du *goût*, ce n'est guères
Que pour la terre et les pierres.
Dinn! dinn! dinn! dinn! Mangeons l'air,
Le roc, les charbons, le fer.

Les faims, tournez. Paissez, faims,
    Le pré des sons!
Attirez le gai venin
    Des liserons;

Les cailloux qu'un pauvre brise,
Les vieilles pierres d'églises,
Les galets, fils des déluges,
Pains couchés aux vallées grises!

Mes faims, c'est les bouts d'air noir;
    L'azur sonneur;
—C'est l'estomac qui me tire.
    C'est le malheur.

Sur terre ont paru les feuilles:
Je vais aux chairs de fruit blettes.
Au sein du sillon je cueille
La doucette et la violette.

Ma faim, Anne, Anne!
Fuis sur ton âne.

Août 1872

Feasts of Hunger

Anne, Anne, my hunger,
flee on your donkey.

If I have a *taste*, it's only for
the earth and for the stones.
Dinn! Dinn! Dinn! Dinn! Let us eat air,
and rock, and coal, and iron.

Turn, my hungers! Graze, my hungers
    on fields of bran.
Suck out the brilliant poisons
    of the bindweed!

The rocks an old man splits,
the old walls of churches,
loaves of stones in valleys,
boulders, offspring of floods!

My hungers, they are bits of black air;
    blue trumpeter;
my stomach draws me there, there!
    It is despair.

Leaves have sprouted on earth!
I seek the soft flesh of fruit.
In a trench's heart, I root
through the mâche and violets.

Anne, Anne, my hunger!
flee on your donkey.

AUGUST, 1872

Les corbeaux

Seigneur, quand froide est la prairie,
Quand, dans les hameaux abattus,
Les longs angelus se sont tus...
Sur la nature défleurie
Faites s'abattre des grands cieux
Les chers corbeaux délicieux.

Armée étrange aux cris sévères,
Les vents froids attaquent vos nids!
Vous, le long des fleuves jaunis,
Sur les routes aux vieux calvaires,
Sur les fossés et sur les trous
Dispersez-vous, ralliez-vous!

Par milliers, sur les champs de France,
Où dorment des morts d'avant-hier,
Tournoyez, n'est-ce pas, l'hiver,
Pour que chaque passant repense!
Sois donc le crieur du devoir,
O notre funèbre oiseau noir!

Mais, saints du ciel, en haut du chêne,
Mât perdu dans le soir charmé,
Laissez les fauvettes de mai
Pour ceux qu'au fond du bois enchaîne,
Dans l'herbe d'où l'on ne peut fuir,
La défaite sans avenir.

The Crows

Lord, when the meadow is frozen
—when, in exhausted villages,
they've silenced the Angelus—
make swoop down to me, here below,
to pastures that bloom no longer,
my mad, entertaining crows.

A strange army with severe cries,
cold winds lay siege to your aeries!
You, along the yellow reeds,
by roads where cavalries once plied,
over furrows, over bare holes,
scatter now! And then—go bawl!

In your thousands, throughout France,
over fields where the dead retire,
squawk about in the winter!
Spark the passerby's remembrance!
Indulge in this act of Duty
—be an avian sentry.

Saints of the sky, atop an oak
mast tilting in enchanted night,
let the May warblers delight
for those who—listening in groves
in grass they can't escape—endure,
defeated, with no future.

1872

Michel et Christine

Zut alors si le soleil quitte ces bords!
Fuis, clair déluge! Voici l'ombre des routes.
Dans les saules, dans la vieille cour d'honneur
L'orage d'abord jette ses larges gouttes.

O cent agneaux, de l'idylle soldats blonds,
Des aqueducs, des bruyères amaigries,
Fuyez! plaine, déserts, prairie, horizons
Sont à la toilette rouge de l'orage!

Chien noir, brun pasteur dont le manteau s'engouffre,
Fuyez l'heure des éclairs supérieurs;
Blond troupeau, quand voici nager ombre et soufre,
Tâchez de descendre à des retraits meilleurs.

Mais moi, Seigneur! voici que mon Esprit vole,
Après les cieux glacés de rouge, sous les
Nuages célestes qui courent et volent
Sur cent Solognes longues comme un railway.

Voilà mille loups, mille graines sauvages
Qu'emporte, non sans aimer les liserons,
Cette religieuse après-midi d'orage
Sur l'Europe ancienne où cent hordes iront!

Après, le clair de lune! partout la lande,
Rougissant et leurs fronts aux cieux noirs, les guerriers
Chevauchent lentement leurs pâles coursiers!
Les cailloux sonnent sous cette fière bande!

—Et verrai-je le bois jaune et le val clair,
L'Épouse aux yeux bleus, l'homme au front rouge, —ô Gaule,
Et le blanc agneau Pascal, à leurs pieds chers,
—Michel et Christine,—et Christ!—fin de l'Idylle.

Michel and Christine

What a disaster if the sun leaves these shores!
Be off, wild storm! Here is the shade of the roads.
In the old noble courtyards, in the willows,
the thunderstorm sheds its first heavy droplets.

Oh, hundred lambs, blonde soldiers of the idylls,
escape the aqueducts, the dried up heather
in plots! Plains, deserts, prairies and horizons
are being purged by the red wash of the storms!

Brown shepherd in your billowing cloak, black dog,
escape if you can the hour of proud lightning.
As darkness and suffering press in, blonde flock
descend and scramble to your cozy lodgings!

Oh, Lord! See, there is my spirit that escapes
beneath the reddening icy skies, under
celestial clouds as they course and surmount
a hundred Solanges, long as a railway.

Behold a thousand wolves, a thousand wild seeds,
who are drawn, not without kissing the bindweed,
away by this religious afternoon of storms
to old Europe where a hundred hordes will teem.

Afterwards—the moonlight! Over all the land,
reddened warriors, faces toward the black skies,
stride by slowly atop their pale stallions!
The pebbles make a din beneath these proud men!

—And will I see the yellow woods and bright valley,
the Bride with blue eyes, the red-browed Man—oh Gaul,
and bowing at their feet the white paschal lamb
—Michel and Christine!—Christ!—End of Idyll.

1872

"Plates-bandes d'amarantes..."

Juillet.   Bruxelles
            Boulevart du Régent.

Plates-bandes d'amarantes jusqu'à
L'agréable palais de Jupiter.
—Je sais que c'est Toi, qui, dans ces lieux,
Mêles ton Bleu presque de Sahara!

Puis, comme rose et sapin du soleil
Et liane ont ici leurs jeux enclos,
Cage de la petite veuve!...
                        Quelles
Troupes d'oiseaux! o iaio, iaio!...

—Calmes maisons, anciennes passions!
Kiosque de la Folle par affection.
Après les fesses des rosiers, balcon
Ombreux et très-bas de la Juliette.

—La Juliette, ça rappelle l'Henriette,
Charmante station du chemin de fer
Au cœur d'un mont comme au fond d'un verger
Où mille diables bleus dansent dans l'air!

Banc vert où chante au paradis d'orage,
Sur la guitare, la blanche Irlandaise.
Puis de la salle à manger guyanaise
Bavardage des enfants et des cages.

Fenêtre du duc qui fais que je pense
Au poison des escargots et du buis
Qui dort ici-bas au soleil.
                        Et puis
C'est trop beau! trop! Gardons notre silence.

"Amaranth flowerbeds..."

July.   Brussels
         Boulevart du Régent.

Amaranth flowerbeds that ascend
to the pleasant palace of Jupiter
—I know it is Thee, who in this scene
mingles your near-blue Sahara!

Then, as the sun's rose and pine
and creepers have their play snagged here,
the small window's prison!
                              What
flocks of birds, o iaio, iaio!...

—Sleepy houses, classic passions,
chateaus of the belle dame mad
in love! From the cheeks of roses,
the balcony, shadowy and low, of Juliet.

—The Juliet, she recalls The Henriette,
charming station dressed in iron
in an Alp's heart, as in an orchard,
—a thousand blue fiends dance on air!

Green bench where, in monsoon's Eden,
the white Irish girl hums with guitar.
Then, from Guyanese dinettes,
the blabber of tykes and corrals.

The duke's widow who makes me think
of poisoned snails, of boxwood
that laze in the sun.
                         And then—
It's so cool! cool!—Let us be silent.

—Boulevart sans mouvement ni commerce,
Muet, tout drame et toute comédie,
Réunion des scènes infinie,
Je te connais et t'admire en silence.

—Boulevart without flow or commerce,
mute, all drama and comedy,
and an infinite rehash of scenes
where I know you, admire you, in silence.

1872

"Entends comme brame…"

Entends comme brame
près des acacias
en avril la rame
viride du pois!

Dans sa vapeur nette,
vers Phoebé! tu vois
s'agiter la tête
de saints d'autrefois…

Loin des claires meules
des caps, des beaux toits,
ces chers Anciens veulent
ce philtre sournois…

Or ni fériale
ni astrale! n'est
la brume qu'exhale
ce nocturne effet.

Néanmoins ils restent,
—Sicile, Allemagne,
dans ce brouillard triste
et blêmi, justement!

"Hear how it knells…"

Hear how it knells
near the acacias
in April—the green
shoot of the pea!

In its clear haze
toward Phoebe, you see,
shaking, the heads
of yesterday's saints…

Far from the bright stacks
of the capes, the nice roofs,
these Ancients crave
this sly aphrodisiac…

The fog exhaled by
this nocturnal effect
is a gold neither everyday
nor astral!

Nevertheless, they remain—
Sicily, Germany,
in this sad and pale
miasma, precisely!

1872

Honte

Tant que la lame n'aura
Pas coupé cette cervelle,
Ce paquet blanc vert et gras
À vapeur jamais nouvelle,

(Ah! Lui, devrait couper son
Nez, sa lèvre, ses oreilles,
Son ventre! et faire abandon
De ses jambes! ô merveille!)

Mais, non, vrai, je crois que tant
Que pour sa tête la lame
Que les cailloux pour son flanc
Que pour ses boyaux la flamme

N'auront pas agi, l'enfant
Gêneur, la si sotte bête,
Ne doit cesser un instant
De ruser et d'être traître

Comme un chat des Monts-Rocheux;
D'empuantir toutes sphères!
Qu'à sa mort pourtant, ô mon Dieu!
S'élève quelque prière!

Shame

As long as the blade has not
cut off that brain—that white
green, fatty, fleshy knot
whose vapor is a tad ripe,

(Ah! HE should cut off his
nose, lips, ears, his eyeballs,
and set aside his limbs!
Oh, what fun—and a marvel!)

—But truly, I believe that
if the blade to his neck,
if the pebble to his side,
if the fire to his stomach

have done nothing, this tiresome
child, this so stupid beast,
must never a moment
cease to betray and cheat,

and, like a Rocky Mountain cat,
to stink up every sphere!
Still, when he dies, oh my God!
may there rise a small prayer!

1872

Memoire

I.

L'eau claire; comme le sel des larmes d'enfance,
l'assaut au soleil des blancheurs des corps de femmes;
la soie, en foule et de lys pur, des oriflammes
sous les murs dont quelque pucelle eut la défense;

l'ébat des anges;—non... le courant d'or en marche,
meut ses bras, noirs, et lourds, et frais surtout, d'herbe. Elle
sombre, avant le Ciel bleu pour ciel-de-lit, appelle
pour rideaux l'ombre de la colline et de l'arche.

II.

Eh! l'humide carreau tend ses bouillons limpides!
L'eau meuble d'or pâle et sans fond les couches prêtes.
Les robes vertes et déteintes des fillettes
font les saules, d'où sautent les oiseaux sans brides.

Plus pure qu'un louis, jaune et chaude paupière
le souci d'eau—ta foi conjugale, à l'Épouse!—
au midi prompt, de son terne miroir, jalouse
au ciel gris de chaleur la Sphère rose et chère.

III.

Madame se tient trop debout dans la prairie
prochaine où neigent les fils du travail; l'ombrelle
aux doigts; foulant l'ombelle; trop fière pour elle
des enfants lisant dans la verdure fleurie

leur livre de maroquin rouge! Hélas, Lui, comme
mille anges blancs qui se séparent sur la route,
s'éloigne par delà la montagne! Elle, toute
froide, et noire, court! après le départ de l'homme!

Memory

I.

A clear water; like the salt of the tears of children,
the whiteness of women's bodies assaults the sun;
a flock of silk banners, pure lilies gathered on
the heights of castles that a maid once safeguarded;

the frolics of angels; no... a golden current
flows, swinging—arms black, thick, quite cold—with grasses. It
sinks, before a canopy of blue Sky, entreats
the shadows of the hill and arches for curtains.

II.

Ah! the humid glass tiles extend their trails of broth!
Water fills tidy beds with pale, bottomless gold.
Garments, long faded and green, of innocent girls
are willows from which flocks of gossipy birds bound.

Purer than a gold coin, a warm, yellow eyelid,
a marsh marigold—oh, Spouse! in faithful marriage!—
at each high noon, jealous, a secret war wages
with the fabled rose Sphere, dead in the sky's gray heat.

III.

Straight as a board, Madame keeps watch in the pasture
where snowy tendrils of labor fall; parasol
in hand; trampling the crops of umbel; too proud for
her, children reading books hidden in deep verdure,

—books bound with Moroccan leather! And behold: He,
like a thousand white angels parting upon the road,
runs off into the mountains! So that leaves She—cold
and sullen. —But she bolts—after the fleeing beast!

IV.

Regret des bras épais et jeunes d'herbe pure!
Or des lunes d'avril au cœur du saint lit! Joie
des chantiers riverains à l'abandon, en proie
aux soirs d'août qui faisaient germer ces pourritures.

Qu'elle pleure à présent sous les remparts! l'haleine
des peupliers d'en haut est pour la seule brise.
Puis, c'est la nappe, sans reflets, sans source, grise:
un vieux, dragueur, dans sa barque immobile, peine.

V.

Jouet de cet œil d'eau morne, Je n'y puis prendre,
oh! canot immobile! oh! bras trop courts! ni l'une
ni l'autre fleur: ni la jaune qui m'importune,
là; ni la bleue, amie à l'eau couleur de cendre.

Ah! la poudre des saules qu'une aile secoue!
Les roses des roseaux dès longtemps dévorées!
Mon canot, toujours fixe; et sa chaîne tirée
au fond de cet œil d'eau sans bords,—à quelle boue?

IV.

Longing for the stiff young arms of the pure wild grass!
Gold of April moons, crux of a saintly berth! Joy,
of abandoned, creaking boatyards, a prey to ploys
of hot, August nights—nurseries for rotting mass.

Now, let her sob beneath the ramparts. Blown vapors
of the poplars above provide the only breeze.
Later, there is the sheen—gray, mirrorless, sere:
an old man in a still boat, a Dredger, who toils.

V.

Toy of this sad lake's eye, this I cannot retrieve
—oh, immobile barque! oh, the arms too short!—neither
this nor the other bloom: yellow one that needles
me, there! or the blue friendly one in darkened lees.

Ah! the powder of willows set loose by loud wings!
Roses of the reeds ingested before my time!
And my barque still mired; and its chain stuck, still entwined
in what mud in this deep eye of rain, unending?

1872

"Le loup criait ..."

Le loup criait sous les feuilles
En crachant les belles plumes
De son repas de volailles:
Comme lui je me consume.

Les salades, les fruits
N'attendent que la cuillette;
Mais l'araignée de la haie
Ne mange que des violettes.

Que je dorme! que je bouille
Aux autels de Salomon.
Le bouillon court sur la rouille,
Et se mêle au Cédron.

"The wolf cried..."

The wolf cried in the forest
gnawing on breast of fowl,
and coughed up the finest plumes
—like him, I consume myself.

Lettuce, fruit and legumes
aspire to the harvest;
but spiders in the hedges
like only to gnaw on violets.

Let me sleep, let me boil at
the shrine of Solomon!
Boiling broth streams down rust
and merges with the Kedron.

1872

"Qu'est-ce pour nous, mon cœur..."

Qu'est-ce pour nous, mon cœur que les nappes de sang
Et de braise, et mille meurtres, et les longs cris
De rage, sanglots de tout enfer renversant
Tout ordre; et l'Aquilon encor sur les debris

Et toute vengeance? Rien!...—Mais si, tout encor,
Nous la voulons! Industriels, princes, sénats,
Périssez! puissance, justice, histoire, à bas!
Ça nous est dû. Le sang! le sang! la flamme d'or!

Tout à la guerre, à la vengeance, à la terreur,
Mon Esprit! Tournons dans la Morsure: Ah! passez,
Républiques de ce monde! Des empereurs,
Des régiments, des colons, des peuples, assez!

Qui remuerait les tourbillons de feu furieux,
Que nous et ceux que nous nous imaginons frères?
A nous! Romanesques amis: ça va nous plaire.
Jamais nous ne travaillerons, ô flots de feux!

Europe, Asie, Amérique, disparaissez.
Notre marche vengeresse a tout occupé,
Cités et campagnes!—Nous serons écrasés!
Les volcans sauteront! et l'océan frappé...

Oh! mes amis!—mon cœur, c'est sûr, ils sont des frères:
Noirs inconnus, si nous allions! allons! allons!
O malheur! je me sens frémir, la vieille terre,
Sur moi de plus en plus à vous! la terre fond,

Ce n'est rien! j'y suis! j'y suis toujours.

"What does it matter, my heart..."

What does it matter, my heart? —Blankets of blood,
hot coals, a thousand murders, piercing cries
of rage, satanic wailing that overturns
order—a north wind that cycles debris?

What of vengeance? Nothing! Yes, but even so,
we want it! Industrialists, lords, senates,
perish! Power, justice, history—burn now!
We've earned it! Blood! blood! the retributive fires!

Everyone to war, to vengeance, to terror
—my spirit! Let us gnash in the maw! Vanish,
republics of this world! Oh, you emperors,
soldiers, patriots, colonists—perish!

Who would stir up the winds of furious fire
but us, and those we christen are our brothers?
Romantic friends, it's up to us—our pleasure
will be to never work! Oh, enabling fire!

Europe, Asia, America—disappear!
Our march of vengeance has occupied all earth
—city and country! We will be overturned,
the volcanoes will burst! the oceans hemorrhaged...

Oh, my friends! My heart, I'm sure, they are brothers,
dark unknowns—if we go off? Let's go! Let's go!
Oh, tragedy! I feel myself quake, old earth
upon me—more and more yours! the earth dissolves...

It is nothing! I am here! I am still here.

1872

"O saisons, ô châteaux..."

O saisons, ô châteaux
Quelle âme est sans défauts?

O saisons, ô châteaux!

J'ai fait la magizue étude
Du Bonheur, que nul n'élude.

O vive lui, chaque fois
Que chante son coq gaulois.

Mais je n'aurai plus d'envie
Il s'est chargé de ma vie.

Ce charme! il prit âme et corps,
Et dispersa tous efforts.

Que comprendre à ma parole?
Il fait qu'elle fuie et vole!

ô saisons ô châteaux

"Oh seasons, oh castles..."

Oh seasons, oh castles,
What soul is without fault?

Oh seasons, oh castles!

I've studied the magic runes
of Joy one can't elude.

Oh, let it live, each dawn
when its Gallic cock crows!

I will have no desires...
It has commandeered my life!

That hex! It took soul and flesh,
and erased their efforts!

Who understands my words?
...It has swirled them into clouds!

Oh seasons, oh castles!

1872

8: LAST POEM

"On a faim dans la chambrée..."

On a faim dans la chambrée—
      C'est vrai...
   Émanations, explosions. Un génie:
   "Je suis le gruère!—
Lefêbvre: "Keller!"
Le Génie: "Je suis le Brie!"
Les soldats coupent sur leur pain:
      "C'est la vie!
Le Génie. —"Je suis le Roquefort!
   —"Ça s'ra not' mort!....
   —Je suis le gruère
   Et le Brie!....etc.
   —Valse
On nous a joints, Lefêvbre et moi... etc.

"One gets hungry..."

One gets hungry in this old barracks room—
   It is true...
  Ejaculations, curses. One genius:
  "I am the Gruyère!—
Lefêbvre: "Beer garden!"
One genius: "I am the Brie!"
The soldiers gnaw away at day old bread.
    "Fuck this shit!"
One genius: "I am the Roquefort!
  —"Is this life?...
  —I am the Gruyère
  and the Brie!... etc.
  —Waltz
We're peas in a pod, Lefêbvre and I... etc.

1875

9: FRAGMENTS AND DOGGEREL

"Oh! si les cloches sont de bronze…"

Oh! si les cloches sont de bronze,
Nos cœurs sont pleins de désespoir!
En juin mil huit cent soixante-onze,
Trucidés par un être noir,
Nous Jean Baudry, nous Jean Balouche,
Ayant accompli nos souhaits,
Mourûmes en ce clocher louche
En abominant Desdouets!…

"Oh, if the clocks are all of bronze..."

Oh, if the clocks are all of bronze
our hearts are full of despair!
In June, eighteen seventy-one,
bumped off by a black killer,
we Jean Balouche, we Jean Baudry,
having aced our bucket lists,
croaked in this infamous belfry
with loathing for Desdouets!

1871

Vers pour les lieux

"De ce siège si mal tourné..."

De ce siège si mal tourné
Qu'il fait s'embrouiller nos entrailles,
Le trou dut être maçonné
Par de véritables canailles

    Albert Mérat
    Paris, 1872

"Quand le fameux Tropmann..."

Quand le fameux Tropmann détruisit Henri Kink
Cet assassin avait dû s'asseoir sur ce siège
Car le con de Badingue et le con d'Henri V
Sont bien dignes vraiment de cet état de siège.

    Paris, 1872

Toilet Stall Verse

"About this seat so poorly made..."

About this seat so poorly made
that it twists intestines in knots—
the hole most clearly had been shaped
by veritable idiots.

    Albert Mérat
    Paris, 1872

"When the infamous Tropmann..."

When the infamous Tropmann destroyed Henri Klink,
the killer must have spread his ass upon this seat,
for the cunt of Badingue, cunt of Henry the Fifth
would truly be worthy of this seat's state of siege.

    Paris, 1872

"Il pleut doucement..."

Il pleut doucement sur la ville.

"It rains softly..."

It rains softly on the city.

"Vouz avez menti..."

. . . . .Vous avez
Menti, sur mon fémur, vous avez menti, fauve
Apôtre! Vous voulez faire des décavés
De nous? Vous voudriez peler notre front chauve?
Mais moi, j'ai deux fémurs bistournés et gravés!
. . . .

Parce que vous suintez tous les jours au collège
Sur vos collets d'habit de quoi faire un beignet,
Que vous êtes un masque à dentiste, au manège
Un cheval épilé qui bave en un cornet,
Vous croyez effacer mes quarante ans de siège!
. . . .

J'ai mon fémur! J'ai mon fémur! J'ai mon fémur!
C'est cela que depuis quarante ans je bistourne
Sur le bord de ma chaise aimée en noyer dur;
L'impression du bois pour toujours y séjourne;
Et quand j'apercevrai, moi, ton organe impur,
A tous tes abonnés, pitre, à tes abonnées,
Pertractant cet organe avachi de leurs mains, [...]
Je ferai retoucher, pour tous les lendemains,
Ce fémur travaillé depuis quarante années!

"You have lied..."

. . . . .You have lied,
on my femur, you have lied—you beastly, crude
apostle! Do you want to turn us into caved-
in men? Would you like to scalp our bald, fraying heads?
—But I have, twisted and engraved, two femurs!
. . . .

Because, each day at school, your sweat steams in buckets
over your collar, enough to fry a fritter,
and you ape the part of a dentist, on a horse
from the riding school, bald and frothing at the bit—
you think to erase my forty years in office!
. . . .

I have a femur! I have a femur! A femur
I have! That's what I've kneaded these forty years
on the edge of my devoted walnut chair
—the impressions on the wood will always be there.
And I, when I behold your organ so impure,
and all of your subscribers—you hack!—subscribers
fondling that impudent organ in their claws, [...]
I shall touch them, for an infinite tomorrow,
with this femur that's been driven for forty years!

Bribes

1.

Au pied des sombres murs, battant les maigres chiens...

2.

Derrière tressautait en des hoquets grotesques,
Une rose avalée au ventre du portier...

3.

Brune, elle avait seize ans quand on la maria
. . . .
. . . .
Car elle aime d'amour son fils de dix-sept ans.

4.

....Sont-ce
.....(des tonneaux?).......qu'on défonce?
....Non!
C'est un chef cuisinier ronflant comme un basson.

5.

      Oh! les vignettes pérennelles!

6.

..........Parmi les ors, les quartz, les porcelaines,
......................................un pot de nuit banal,
Reliquaire indécent des vieilles châtelaines,
Courbe ses flancs honteux sur l'acajou royal.

7.

Et le poète soùl engueulait l'Univers!

Scraps

1.

At the foot of dark walls, beating the skinny dogs...

2.

Convulsing with foul hiccups behind his waistcoat,
a swallowed rose in the belly of a porter...

3.

A brunette, she was married off at just sixteen
. . . .
. . . .
Because she deeply loved her son of seventeen.

4.

....Is it
.....(the casks?).....being smashed in?
....No!
It is just the head chef, snoring like a bassoon.

5.

Oh! the perrennial vignettes!

6.

..........Among the gold, quartz and porcelein things,
......................................a banal chamberpot,
obscene reliquary of aging chatelaines,
curves its vile sides on the royal mahagony.

7.

And the drunken poet bawls out the Universe!

La plainte de épiciers

Qu'il entre au magasin, quand la lune miroite
    À ses vitrages bleus,
Qu'il empoigne à nos yeux la chicorée en boîte.

The Complaint of Grocers

Let him enter this small store when the moon shimmers
    in the blue window panes,
—let him pinch, before our eyes, tins of chicory.

10: LETTERS OF THE SEER

À Georges Izambard

Charleville, 13 mai 1871

Cher Monsieur!

Vous revoilà professeur. On se doit à la Société, m'avez-vous dit; vous faites partie des corps enseignants: vous roulez dans la bonne ornière.—Moi aussi, je suis le principe: je me fais cyniquement *entretenir*; je déterre d'anciens imbéciles de collège: tout ce que je puis inventer de bête, de sale, de mauvais, en action et en parole, je le leur livre: on me paie en bocks et en filles. *Stat mater dolorosa, dum pendet filius.*—Je me dois à la Société, c'est juste,—et j'ai raison.—Vous aussi, vous avez raison, pour aujourd'hui. Au fond, vous ne voyez en votre principe que poésie subjective: votre obstination à regagner le râtelier universitaire,—pardon!—le prouve. Mais vous finirez toujours comme un satisfait qui n'a rien fait, n'ayant rien voulu faire. Sans compter que votre poésie subjective sera toujours horriblement fadasse. Un jour, j'espère,—bien d'autres espèrent la même chose,—je verrai dans votre principe la poésie objective, je la verrai plus sincèrement que vous ne le feriez!—Je serai un travailleur: c'est l'idée qui me retient, quand les colères folles me poussent vers la bataille de Paris—où tant de travailleurs meurent pourtant encore tandis que je vous écris! Travailler maintenant, jamais, jamais; je suis en grève.

Maintenant, je m'encrapule le plus possible. Pourquoi? Je veux être poète, et je travaille à me rendre *voyant*: vous ne comprendrez pas du tout, et je ne saurais presque vous expliquer. Il s'agit d'arriver à l'inconnu par le dérèglement de *tous les sens*. Les souffrances sont énormes, mais il faut être fort, être né poète, et je me suis reconnu poète. Ce n'est pas du tout ma faute. C'est faux de dire: Je pense: on devrait dire: On me pense.—Pardon du jeu de mots.—

Je est un autre. Tant pis pour le bois qui se trouve violon, et Nargue aux inconscients, qui ergotent sur ce qu'ils ignorent tout à fait!

To Georges Izambard

Charleville, 13 May 1871

Cher Monsieur!

Once again, you are a teacher. You've said that we have a duty to Society; you belong to the teaching profession: you wheel along the right rut. Me too, I am the principle: cynically, I am having myself *kept*; I dig up old imbeciles from school: I give them all I'm able to invent that is stupid, filthy, horrifying, in acts and words; they pay me in beer and girls. S*tat mater dolorosa, dum pendet filius.* —My duty is to Society, that is true—and I am right. —You are right, too, for now. But really, all you see in your principle is subjective poetry: your obstinacy in returning to the university rack—excuse me—proves this. But you will always end up a contented man who has done nothing, wanted to do nothing. Not to mention that your subjective poetry will always be horribly dull. One day, I hope—many others hope the same thing—I will see objective poetry according to your principle, I will see it more sincerely than you would! I will be a worker: this idea restrains me when crazy anger drives me toward the battle of Paris—where so many workers are dying as I write this! Work now? never, never; I am on strike.

Now, I am self-dissipating as much as possible. Why? I want to be a poet, and so I work to make myself a *seer*: you will not understand this at all, and I barely know how to explain it to you. It is about reaching the unknown by the disordering of *all the senses*. The sufferings are enormous, but one has to be strong, have been born a poet, and I know I am a poet. This is not my fault at all. It is wrong to say: I think. One ought to say: I am being thought. Pardon the pun.

I is an other. Too bad for the wood which finds itself a violin, and scorn for the foolhardy who argue over what they know nothing of!

Vous n'êtes pas *Enseignant* pour moi. Je vous donne ceci: est-ce de la satire, comme vous diriez? Est-ce de la poésie? C'est de la fantaisie, toujours.—Mais, je vous en supplie, ne soulignez ni du crayon, ni trop de la pensée:

[Le cœur supplicié]

Ça ne veut pas rien dire.—*Répondez-Moi*: chez M. Deverrière, pour A. R.

Bonjour de cœur,
Art. Rimbaud.

You are not a *Teacher* for me. I send you this: is it satire, as you would say? Is it poetry? It's fantasy, always. —But I beg you, do not underline it with your pencil, nor too much with your thought:

[The Tortured Heart]

This does not mean nothing. —*Answer me*: care of M. Deverrière, for A.R.

A heartfelt hello,
Art. Rimbaud

À Paul Demeny

Charleville, 15 mai 1871   •

J'ai résolu de vous donner une heure de littérature nouvelle. Je commence de suite par un psaume d'actualité:

[Chant de guerre parisien]

—Voici de la prose sur l'avenir de la poésie—

Toute poésie antique aboutit à la poésie grecque; Vie harmonieuse.—De la Grèce au mouvement romantique,—moyen-âge,—il y a des lettrés, des versificateurs. D'Ennius à Théroldus, de Théroldus à Casimir Delavigne, tout est prose rimée, un jeu, avachissement et gloire d'innombrables générations idiotes: Racine est le pur, le fort, le grand.—On eût soufflé sur ses rimes, brouillé ses hémistiches, que le Divin Sot serait aujourd'hui aussi ignoré que le premier venu auteur d'*Origines*.—Après Racine, le jeu moisit. Il a duré deux mille ans!

Ni plaisanterie, ni paradoxe. La raison m'inspire plus de certitudes sur le sujet que n'aurait jamais eu de colères un Jeune-France. Du reste, libre aux *nouveaux*! d'exécrer les ancêtres: on est chez soi et l'on a le temps.

On n'a jamais bien jugé le romantisme; qui l'aurait jugé? Les critiques!! Les romantiques, qui prouvent si bien que la chanson est si peu souvent l'œuvre, c'est-à-dire la pensée chantée *et comprise* du chanteur?

Car Je est un autre. Si le cuivre s'éveille clairon, il n'y a rien de sa faute. Cela m'est évident: j'assiste à l'éclosion de ma pensée: je la regarde, je l'écoute: je lance un coup d'archet: la symphonie fait son remuement dans les profondeurs, ou vient d'un bond sur la scène.

To Paul Demeny

Charleville, 15 May 1871

I've decided to give you an hour of new literature. I begin now with a psalm about current events:

[Parisian War Song]

—Here is some prose on the future of poetry:—

All ancient poetry ended in Greek poetry; harmonious Life. —From Greece to the Romantic movement—Middle Ages—there are men of letters, versifiers. From Ennius to Theroldus, from Theroldus to Casimir Delavigne, it is all rhymed prose, a game, limpness and glory of countless idiotic generations: Racine is the pure, the strong, the great. —Were one to have blown upon his rhymes, mixed up his hemistichs, the Divine Fool would today be as unknown as any old author of *Origins*. —After Racine, the game gets moldy. It has lasted two thousand years!

Neither a joke, nor a paradox. Reason inspires me with more conviction on the subject than Young France ever had in their rages. Besides, the *new ones* are free! to condemn our ancestors: one is home and one has the time.

Romanticism has never been carefully tried; who would have been the judge? The critics!! The Romantics, who prove so obviously that a song is almost never the work, meaning, the singer's sung *and understood* thought.

For I is an other. If brass wakes up a trumpet, it is not its fault. This is obvious to me: I am present at the birth of my thought: I watch it, I listen to it: I draw a stroke of the bow: the symphony stirs in the deeps, or arrives with a leap onto the stage.

Si les vieux imbéciles n'avaient pas trouvé du Moi que la signification fausse, nous n'aurions pas à balayer ces millions de squelettes qui, depuis un temps infini! ont accumulé les produits de leur intelligence borgnesse, en s'en clamant les auteurs!

En Grèce, ai-je dit, vers et lyres *rhythment l'Action*. Après, musique et rimes sont jeux, délassements. L'étude de ce passé charme les curieux: plusieurs s'éjouissent à renouveler ces antiquités:—c'est pour eux. L'intelligence universelle a toujours jeté ses idées, naturellement; les hommes ramassaient une partie de ces fruits du cerveau: on agissait par, on en écrivait des livres: telle allait la marche, l'homme ne se travaillant pas, n'étant pas encore éveillé, ou pas encore dans la plénitude du grand songe. Des fonctionnaires, des écrivains: auteur, créateur, poète, cet homme n'a jamais existé!

La première étude de l'homme qui veut être poète est sa propre connaissance, entière; il cherche son âme, il l'inspecte, il la tente, l'apprend. Dès qu'il la sait, il doit la cultiver; Cela semble simple: en tout cerveau s'accomplit un développement naturel; tant *d'égoïstes* se proclament auteurs; il en est bien d'autres qui s'attribuent leur progrès intellectuel!—Mais il s'agit de faire l'âme monstrueuse: à l'instar des comprachicos, quoi! Imaginez un homme s'implantant et se cultivant des verrues sur le visage.

Je dis qu'il faut être *voyant*, se faire *voyant*.

Le Poète se fait *voyant* par un long, immense et raisonné *dérèglement* de *tous les sens*. Toutes les formes d'amour, de souffrance, de folie; il cherche lui-même, il épuise en lui tous les poisons, pour n'en garder que les quintessences. Ineffable torture où il a besoin de toute la foi, de toute la force surhumaine, où il devient entre tous le grand malade, le grand criminel, le grand maudit,—et le suprême Savant—Car il arrive à l'inconnu! Puisqu'il a cultivé son âme, déjà riche, plus qu'aucun! Il arrive à l'inconnu, et quand, affolé, il finirait par perdre l'intelligence de ses visions, il les a vues! Qu'il crève dans son bondissement par les choses inouïes et innombrables: viendront d'autres horribles travailleurs; ils commenceront par les horizons où l'autre s'est affaissé!

If old imbeciles had not discovered only the false meaning of the Ego, we would not have to sweep away those millions of skeletons which, for times immemorial! have accumulated the fruits of their one-eyed intellects by claiming to be authors!

In Greece, as I have said, verses and lyres *give rhythm to Action*. Later, music and rhymes are games, pastimes. The study of this past delights the curious: many rejoice in reviving those antiquities—it is for them. Universal intelligence has always naturally hurled out its ideas; men picked up a part of these fruits of the mind: people acted through them, wrote books about them: things continued thus, man not working on himself, not yet being awake, or not yet in the fullness of the great dream. Civil servants, writers: author, creator, poet, that man never existed!

The first study of the man who wants to be a poet is the knowledge of himself, complete; he seeks his soul, inspects it, tests it, learns it. As soon as he knows it, he must cultivate it; it seems simple: in every mind a natural development takes place; so many *egoists* proclaim themselves authors; there are many others who attribute to themselves their intellectual progress! — But the soul must be made monstrous: in the manner of the *comprachicos*, if you will! Imagine a man implanting and cultivating warts on his face.

I say one must be a *seer*, make oneself a *seer*.

The Poet makes himself a *seer* by a long, gigantic and rational *disordering* of *all the senses*. All forms of love, suffering, madness; he searches himself, he exhausts all poisons in himself, keeps only their quintessences. Unspeakable torture where he needs all his faith, all of his superhuman strength, where he becomes before all the great patient, the great criminal, the one accursed— and the supreme Scholar!—because he reaches the unknown! Since he cultivated his soul, rich already, more than anyone! He reaches the unknown, and when, alarmed, he ends up by losing the intelligence of his visions, he has seen them! Let him die in his career through unprecedented and unnamable things: other horrible workers will come; they will start from the horizons where the other collapsed!

—La suite à six minutes—

Ici j'intercale un second psaume, *hors du texte*: veuillez tendre une oreille complaisante,—et tout le monde sera charmé.—J'ai l'archet en main, je commence:

[Mes petites amoureuses]

Voilà. Et remarquez bien que, si je ne craignais de vous faire débourser plus de 60 c. de port,—moi pauvre effaré qui, depuis sept mois, n'ai pas tenu un seul rond de bronze!—je vous livrerais encore mes *Amants de Paris*, cent hexamètres, Monsieur, et ma *Mort de Paris*, deux cents hexamètres! —Je reprends:

Donc le poète est vraiment voleur de feu.

Il est chargé de l'humanité, des *animaux* même; il devra faire sentir, palper, écouter ses inventions; si ce qu'il rapporte *de là-bas* a forme, il donne forme: si c'est informe, il donne de l'informe. Trouver une langue;

—Du reste, toute parole étant idée, le temps d'un langage universel viendra! Il faut être académicien,—plus mort qu'un fossile,—pour parfaire un dictionnaire, de quelque langue que ce soit. Des faibles se mettraient *à penser* sur la première lettre de l'alphabet, qui pourraient vite ruer dans la folie!—

Cette langue sera de l'âme pour l'âme, résumant tout, parfums, sons, couleurs, de la pensée accrochant la pensée et tirant. Le poète définirait la quantité d'inconnu s'éveillant en son temps dans l'âme universelle: il donnerait plus—que la formule de sa pensée, que la notation *de sa marche au Progrès*! Enormité devenant norme, absorbée par tous, il serait vraiment *un multiplicateur de progrès*!

Cet avenir sera matérialiste, vous le voyez;—Toujours pleins du *Nombre* et de l'*Harmonie* ces poèmes seront faits pour rester.—Au fond, ce serait encore un peu la Poésie grecque. L'art éternel aurait ses fonctions; comme les

—To be continued in six minutes—

To accompany the text, here I insert a second psalm: please lend a friendly ear—and everyone will be delighted. —The bow is in my hand, I begin:

[My Little Mistresses]

That's that. And note carefully that if I were not afraid of making you spend more than sixty centimes on postage—I poor terrified one who for seven months have not had a single copper!—I would also give you my *Lovers of Paris*, one hundred hexameters, sir, and my *Death of Paris*, two hundred hexameters! —I continue:

Therefore the poet is truly the thief of fire.

He is responsible for humanity, even for the *animals*; he will have to have his own inventions smelt, felt, and heard; if what he brings back *from below* has form, he delivers form; if it is *informe*, he delivers *informe*. A language must be found.

—Moreover, every word being an idea, the time of a universal language will come! One has to be an academician—deader than a fossil—to complete a dictionary in any language whatsoever. The weak would begin *to think* about the first letter of the alphabet, which would rush quickly into madness!

This language will be of the soul for the soul, accounting for all, smells, sounds, colors, of thought catching thought and pulling. The poet would define the amount of the unknown awakening in the universal soul of his time: he would give more—than the formulation of his thought, than the record *of his march toward Progress!* Enormity becoming the norm, absorbed by all, he would really be a *multiplier of progress!*

This future will be materialistic, as you see. —Always filled with *Number* and *Harmony*, these poems will be made to endure. —Basically, it would be

poètes sont citoyens. La Poésie ne rhythmera plus l'action, elle *sera en avant*.

Ces poètes seront! Quand sera brisé l'infini servage de la femme, quand elle vivra pour elle et par elle, l'homme,—jusqu'ici abominable,—lui ayant donné son renvoi, elle sera poète, elle aussi! La femme trouvera de l'inconnu! Ses mondes d'idées différeront-ils des nôtres?—Elle trouvera des choses étranges, insondables, repoussantes, délicieuses; nous les prendrons, nous les comprendrons.

En attendant, demandons aux *poètes* du *nouveau*,—idées et formes. Tous les habiles croiraient bientôt avoir satisfait à cette demande.—Ce n'est pas cela!

Les premiers romantiques ont été *voyants* sans trop bien s'en rendre compte: la culture de leurs âmes s'est commencée aux accidents: locomotives abandonnées, mais brûlantes, que prennent quelque temps les rails.—Lamartine est quelquefois voyant, mais étranglé par la forme vieille.—Hugo, *trop cabochard*, a bien du *vu* dans les derniers volumes: *Les Misérables* sont un vrai *poème*. J'ai *Les châtiments* sous la main; *Stella* donne à peu près la mesure de la *vue* de Hugo. Trop de Belmontet et de Lamennais, de Jéhovahs et de colonnes, vieilles énormités crevées.

Musset est quatorze fois exécrable pour nous, générations douloureuses et prises de visions,—que sa paresse d'ange a insultées! Ô! les contes et les proverbes fadasses! Ô les *Nuits*! Ô *Rolla*, Ô *Namouna*, Ô la *Coupe*! Tout est français, c'est-à-dire haïssable au suprême degré; français, pas parisien! Encore une œuvre de cet odieux génie qui a inspiré Rabelais, Voltaire, Jean La Fontaine; commenté par M. Taine! Printanier, l'esprit de Musset! Charmant, son amour! En voilà, de la peinture à l'émail, de la poésie solide! On savourera longtemps la poésie *française*, mais en France. Tout garçon épicier est en mesure de débobiner une apostrophe Rollaque; tout séminariste en porte les cinq cents rimes dans le secret d'un carnet. A quinze ans, ces élans de passion mettent les jeunes en rut; à seize ans, ils se contentent déjà de les réciter avec *cœur*; à dix-huit ans, à dix-sept même, tout collégien qui a le moyen, fait le *Rolla*, écrit un *Rolla*! Quelques-uns en meurent peut-être encore. Musset

Greek poetry again, somewhat. Eternal art would have its functions; as poets are citizens. Poetry will not give rhythm to action, it *will be in advance.*

These poets will exist! When the endless servitude of woman is broken, when she lives by and for herself, man—until now abominable—having given her her release, she will be a poet, she too! Woman will find the unknown! Will her world of ideas differ from ours? —She will find strange, unfathomable, hideous, delicious things; we will take them, we will understand them.

Meanwhile, let us ask the *poets* for the *new*—ideas and forms. All the clever ones will soon believe they have satisfied the demand. —It is not so!

The first Romantics were *seers* without wholly realizing it: the cultivation of their souls began accidentally: abandoned locomotives, fireboxes still burning, which the rails carry along for some time. —Lamartine is at times a *seer*, but choked by the old form. —Hugo, *too pigheaded*, has *vision* in his last volumes: *Les Misérables* is a real poem. I have *Les Châtiments* by my side; *Stella* gives approximately the extent of Hugo's *vision.* Too many Belmontets and Lamennaises, Jehovahs and colonnades, old exhausted enormities.

Musset is fourteen times loathsome to us, suffering generations seized by visions—insulted by his angelic sloth! O! the insipid tales and proverbs! O the *Nuits*! O *Rolla*, O *Namouna*, O the *Coupe*! It is all French, namely hateful to the highest degree; French, not Parisian! One more work of that odious genius that inspired Rabelais, Voltaire, Jean La Fontaine; with M. Taine's commentary! Springlike, Musset's wit! Charming, his love! Here, enamel painting, solid poetry! *French* poetry will be enjoyed for a long time, but in France. Every grocer's boy is able to reel off a Rollaesque speech; every seminarian carries the five hundred rhymes in secret in his notebook. At fifteen, these bursts of passion make boys horny; at sixteen, they are satisfied to recite them with *heart*; at eighteen, even at seventeen, every schoolboy of middling talent makes a *Rolla*, writes a *Rolla*! Perhaps, some still die from it. Musset could do nothing: there were visions behind

n'a rien su faire: il y avait des visions derrière la gaze des rideaux: il a fermé les yeux. Français, panadif, traîné de l'estaminet au pupitre de collège, le beau mort est mort, et, désormais, ne nous donnons même plus la peine de le réveiller par nos abominations!

Les seconds romantiques sont très *voyants*: Th. Gautier, Lec. de Lisle, Th. de Banville. Mais inspecter l'invisible et entendre l'inouï étant autre chose que reprendre l'esprit des choses mortes, Baudelaire est le premier voyant, roi des poètes, *un vrai Dieu*. Encore a-t-il vécu dans un milieu trop artiste; et la forme si vantée en lui est mesquine: les inventions d'inconnu réclament des formes nouvelles.

Rompue aux formes vieilles, parmi les innocents, A. Renaud,—a fait son *Rolla*,—L. Grandet,—a fait son *Rolla*;—les gaulois et les Musset, G. Lafenestre, Coran, Cl. Popelin, Soulary, L. Salles; les écoliers, Marc, Aicard, Theuriet; les morts et les imbéciles, Autran, Barbier, L. Pichat, Lemoyne, les Deschamps, les Desessarts; les journalistes, L. Cladel, Robert Luzarches, X. de Ricard; les fantaisistes, C. Mendès; les bohèmes; les femmes; les talents, Léon Dierx, Sully-Prudhomme, Coppée,—la nouvelle école, dite parnassienne, a deux voyants, Albert Mérat et Paul Verlaine, un vrai poète.—Voilà.— Ainsi je travaille à me rendre *voyant*.—Et finissons par un chant pieux.

[Accroupissements]

Vous seriez exécrable de ne pas répondre: vite car dans huit jours je serai à Paris, peut-être.

Au revoir. A. Rimbaud.

the curtains' gauze: he closed his eyes. French, starchy pulp, dragged from barroom to schoolroom desk, the beautiful death is dead, and, henceforth, let's not even bother to wake it with our abominations.

The second Romantics are very much *seers*: Th[éophile] Gautier, Lec[onte] de Lisle, Th[éodore] de Banville. But since inspecting the invisible and hearing the unheard-of are different from recovering the spirit of dead things, Baudelaire is the first seer, king of poets, *a real God*! Yet he lived in a too-artistic milieu; and the form so highly praised in him is trivial: inventions of the unknown call for new forms.

Broken-in with old forms, among the innocent, A. Renaud—has written his *Rolla*; L. Grandet has written his *Rolla*; the Gauls and the Mussets, G. Lafenestre, Coran, Cl. Popelin, Soulary, L. Salles; the pupils Marc, Aicard, Theuriet; the dead and the imbeciles, Autran, Barbier, L. Pichat, Lemoyne, the Deschamps, the Des Essarts; the journalists, L. Cladel, Robert Luzarches, X. de Ricard; the fantasists, C. Mendès; les bohemians; the women; the talents, Léon Dierx, Sully-Prudhomme, Coppée—the new school, called Parnassian, has two seers: Albert Mérat and Paul Verlaine, a real poet. — There you are. —So, I work to make myself into a *seer*. —And let's close with a pious hymn.

[Squattings]

You would be loathsome not to answer: quickly, because in a week, I will be in Paris, perhaps.

Goodbye. A.Rimbaud

NOTES ON THE POEMS

The following notes largely concern explanations for particular choices in translation (notably, a few anachronisms), some background information about the composition of the poems, and a few glosses. For the most part, I've refrained from providing information about French history or the individuals named, and I haven't glossed any of the references to mythology. I also don't point out variant readings of particular words in Rimbaud's poems since these are mainly of interest to the scholar. In some cases, Rimbaud dated his poems, and even left notes about where they were written. In these instances, the date appears on both the French and English sides of the page spread. Otherwise, the dates are drawn from scholarship. The many long rows of dots, which can appear to be extended ellipses, appear in Rimbaud's original poems. They simply seem to denote a pause, but often appear in poems that have numbered sections. They don't represent omissions.

1: Early Spring

"It Was Spring"

Though I studied Latin for several years, both in my Catholic prep school and in college, and even published a translation from Virgil's *Aeneid*, I didn't go back to the Latin for this poem. Instead, I wrote this based on previous translations of the poem into English and French.

Sun and Flesh [Credo in Unam]

The earlier, longer version of this poem was titled "Credo in Unam." As noted in the introduction, Rimbaud sent this poem to Théodore De Banville for the final issue of *Le Parnasse contemporain*. Banville never replied. Rimbaud later deleted several passages (which are denoted here by brackets) and retitled the poem "Soleil et chair." I decided to translate this poem into varying 10- and 12-syllable lines since

I found it impossible to preserve the rhyming alexandrines of the original.

Nina's Replies

The quatrains in parentheses are verses that Rimbaud later deleted.

2: First Marches

Caesars' Rages

The "Emperor" here is Napolean III, the nephew of Napoleon Bonaparte. He was the first elected president of France, but installed himself as the Emperor of the French after a self-coup in 1851. From September 5th 1870 until March 19th 1871, Napoleon III and his entourage were living in exile in a castle at Wilhelmshöhe, Germany.

At the Cabaret-Vert

The first shipment of coca plants arrived in Europe in 1859 though the first study of the effects of coca in Europe was published in 1855. The term "cocaine" was coined in Germany in 1860 by a German graduate student, Albert Niemann, after he had successfully isolated the primary alkaloid from the coca leaf. Rimbaud, of course, doesn't use the word "cocaine" in his poem, and it most likely was not used as a recreational drug in 1870.

My Bohemian Life (Fantasy)

Though the "cinema" as we understand it today wasn't invented until 1891 by Thomas Edson, several pre-film animation technologies were available in Europe by the early 19th-century. Among these was the "phénakisticope," invented and marketed in 1833, which required the viewer to rotate a disk with sequential images on it and view them through slits. Despite this, "cinema" is, indeed, an anachronism.

3: Approaching Paris

The Blacksmith

See the introduction for background on this poem. The scarlet cap was worn by revolutionaries during this time.

Parisian War Song

Louis Joseph Ernest Picard (1821–1877) was a French politician. Adolphe Thiers (1797–1877) was a French statesman and historian, and eventually France's second President (after Napoleon III). Though Thiers is credited with expelling the Germans after the Franco-Prussian War, he also gave the order to the army to suppress the Paris Commune.

4: Heresies

The Just Man

The first twenty lines of this poem have been lost. Earlier editions of translations of Rimbaud, such as Oliver Bernard's 1962 *Collected Poems* and Wallace Fowlie's 1966 *Complete Works, Selected Letters*, placed the fragments in the final stanza prior to what is the first stanza here starting "Le Juste restait..." In these editions, the last line of the poem is "Lé-chant son flanc d'où pend une entraille emportée." I've followed the more recent practice (for instance in the revised edition of the Fowlie translations, updated and revised by Seth Whidden and published in 2005) of grouping the fragments into a final stanza for the poem. I've gone with Whidden's suggestions regarding what the missing letters and words might be. While many consider the target of this poem to be pious Churchmen, some speculate that the "just man" is Victor Hugo.

5: The Seer

The Stolen Heart

Three versions of this poem exist. "Le coeur supplicié" ("The Tortured Heart") was sent to Georges Izambard on May 13th 1871, "Le coeur du pitre" ("The Fool's Heart") to Paul Demeny on June 10th of the same year. "Le coeur volé" ("The Stolen Heart") was recopied by Verlaine in late 1871 or early 1872. Most of the alterations were a matter of word choices, though it's notable that "vesprée" ("vespers") appears in the earlier drafts in the line concerning the "fresques"—the soldiers made drawings during vespers—in contrast to the appeal Rimbaud makes to heretical magic, "Ô flots abracadabrantesques." I changed "frescoes" to "cartoons" since they are described as "ithyphallic."

Vowels

See the introduction for my notes on this poem.

What Is Said to the Poet Concerning Flowers

See the introduction for my notes on this poem.

6: Poems from the "Album Zutique"

This section contains Rimbaud's contribution to the "Album Zutique" which I describe briefly in the introduction. For the most part, the poems are parodies, often obscene, of well-known poets of the day; the name that appears after the poem is the writer being targeted. The poets parodied each other as well. Occasionally, Rimbaud would initial his entries, other times not. Another favorite target was Napoleon III; "Eugenie" in "The Old Man of the Old Woman!" was his wife. The last three poems in this section did not appear in the album.

Idol. Sonnet to the Asshole

See the introduction for background on this poem.

"I occupied a third class car..."

While no name appears below this entry, Rimbaud was clearly parodying one of his favorite targets, the poet François Copée (1842–1908). Altogether, Rimbaud wrote nine parodies of Copée.

Crude Jokes — 2. Paris

This poem is nearly entirely composed of proper names. It seems to be a celebration of Paris, including the names of celebrities, artists and shop owners, but embraces a darker side with the mention of the murderer Jean-Baptiste Troppmann and his victims Jean Kinck and Kinck's eldest son, Gustave. The phrase "Enghiens Chez soi!" ("Enghiens in the home!") refers to an advertisement for mineral salts that Rimbaud was slightly obsessed with—he repeats the reference in a footnote to "The child who picked up bullets...," his last Copée parody. Rather than gloss all of the references, I decided to try to write a similar homage to Los Angeles, where I now live.

The Old Man of the Old Woman!

See note at the head of this section.

7: After the Rains

Comedy of Thirst — 4. The Poor Dream.

I wasn't able to match the syllable counts of Rimbaud's verses, so I more or less made up my own verse form.

Shame

It's unclear to whom Rimbaud is referring to with the word "Lui." The word is capitalized, which could suggest that "Lui" is a reference to the Christian God. Rimbaud doesn't always capitalize the first word after a poetic apostrophe (see, for example, "Age D'or").

Memory

Rimbaud capitalizes "Lui" here, and is clearly referring to his father, or some poetic evocation of him. "Elle," the mother, is likewise capitalized, but simply because it appears after an exclamation point. I've tried to make clear in my translation that "She" should be capitalized. The third element in this trio, "Je" in the last section, is capitalized in Rimbaud's poem. Given that we capitalize "I" in English, I placed a definite article in front of "I" to signify Rimbaud's choice.

8: Last Poem

"One gets hungry in this old barracks room..."

See the introduction for background on this poem.

9: Fragments and Doggerel

"Oh, if the clocks are all of bronze..."

Jean Baudry was a pen name Rimbaud occasionally used. Jean Balouche was a name his friend, Ernest Delahaye, occasionally adopted. Desdouets was a headmaster they clearly didn't like.

Toilet Stall Verse

The last phrase of the second poem, "état de siège," seems to be a play on the two meanings of the word "siège." Taken alone, the word can mean "seat" (not just the place where one sits, but in other senses such as the "seat of power"). The phrase "état de siège" (which Rimbaud uses as the title of one his "Zutique" poems) means, quite unambiguously, a "state of siege." This pun, naturally, is impossible to reproduce in English, but I quite like my solution.

"It rains softly..."

See the introduction for background on this poem.

Scraps

"Bribes" was the title earlier French editors of Rimbaud used for his collected frag-
ments. I've pulled some of those fragments, such as the short poem "Oh, if the clocks
are all of bronze...," and given them their own pages. I've tried to arrange what re-
mained artfully so that these "Scraps" can be read as a (terribly elliptical) imagistic
poem. "L'Univers" was the name of a bar Rimbaud frequented.

10: Letters of the Seer

"Stat mater dolorosa, dum pendet filius" is Rimbaud's misremembering of the open-
ing lines to the 13th-century hymn "Stabat Mater." "Stabat Mater dolorosa iuxta
crucem lacrimosa dum pendebat Filius" can be translated as "The grieving Mother
stood weeping beside the cross where her Son was hanging."

The "comprachicos," which can be translated as "child-buyers," were an invention of
Victor Hugo's in his novel *The Man Who Laughs*. The "comprachicos" would raise
children, slowly mutilating them so that they later could be displayed as freaks:
"The Comprachicos worked on man as the Chinese work on trees. A sort of fantastic
stunted thing left their hands; it was ridiculous and wonderful. They could touch up
a little being with such skill that its father could not have recognized it. Sometimes
they left the spine straight and remade the face. Children destined for tumblers had
their joints dislocated in a masterly manner; thus gymnasts were made. Not only
did the Comprachicos take away his face from the child; they also took away his
memory. At least, they took away all they could of it; the child had no consciousness
of the mutilation to which he had been subjected."

"I would also give you my *Lovers of Paris*, one hundred hexameters, sir, and my
Death of Paris, two hundred hexameters!" These poems most likely never existed.
Rimbaud is merely mocking the types of poems that were being churned out by
late-Romantics and Parnassians during his time.

Rolla was a long poem by Alfred de Musset published in 1833 that was often imi-
tated.

See the introduction for further discussion of these letters and notes on my translation of them.

INDEX OF FRENCH TITLES

INDEX OF ENGLISH TITLES

ISBN: 978-1-7343176-1-9
Library of Congress Control Number: 2020950481

Published in 2021 by Kenning Editions

Distributed by Small Press Distribution
1341 Seventh St., Berkeley, CA 94710
Spdbooks.org

Cover: Faride Mereb

Frontispiece: Pierre-Ambrose Richebourg, *Barricades de la Commune, avril 71. Coin de la place Hotel de Ville & de la rue de Rivoli* (1871)

Interior composition: Patrick Durgin
Set in Halyard by Eben Sorkin, Joshua Darden, and Lucas Sharp, and Miller by Matthew Carter.

This book was made possible in part by the supporters of Kenning Editions: Alan Bernheimer, Jay Besemer, Mark Booth, Joel Craig, Ian Dreiblatt, Joseph Giardini, Katherine M. Hedeen, Krystal Languell, Joslyn Layne, Olivia Lott, Pamela Lu, Olivia DiNapoli, Thomas Troolin, and The John A. Hartford Foundation.

Kenning Editions is a 501c3 non-profit, independent literary publisher investigating the relationships of aesthetic quality to political commitment. Consider donating or subscribing: Kenningeditions.com/shop/donation

Juana I, by Ana Arzoumanian, translated by Gabriel Amor

Waveform, by Amber DiPietra and Denise Leto

Style, by Dolores Dorantes, translated by Jen Hofer

PQRS, by Patrick Durgin

The Pine-Woods Notebook, by Craig Dworkin

Propagation, by Laura Elrick

Tarnac, a preparatory act, by Jean-Marie Gleize, translated by Joshua Clover with Abigail Lang and Bonnie Roy

The Chilean Flag, by Elvira Hernández, translated by Alec Schumacher

título / title, by Legna Rodríguez Iglesias, translated by Katherine M. Hedeen

Stage Fright: Selected Plays from San Francisco Poets Theater, by Kevin Killian

The Kenning Anthology of Poets Theater: 1945-1985, edited by Kevin Killian and David Brazil

The Grand Complication, by Devin King

There Three, by Devin King

Insomnia and the Aunt, by Tan Lin

Dream of Europe: selected seminars and interviews: 1984-1992, by Audre Lorde, edited by Mayra Rodríguez Castro

KENNING EDITIONS NFP IS A 501 (C) (3), NON-PROFIT PUBLIC CHARITY AND CONTRIBUTIONS ARE TAX DEDUCTIBLE.

KENNINGEDITIONS.COM